Miracles
On My Doorstep

Immigrating To America
Faith Finds Freedom

Lorraine Snider-Hanley

and

Linda Kaye

LINDA KAYE
INTERNATIONAL, INC.

Published by Linda Kaye International Inc. 2052 Bundy Drive #1007 West Los Angeles, CA 90025. (310) 592-2817 www.MiraclesOnMyDoorstep.com

DISCLAIMER AND/OR LEGAL NOTICES

ISBN: 978-1-7379173-1-1 (Print)

ISBN: 978-1-7379173-0-4 (eBook)

PRINTED IN THE UNITED STATES OF AMERICA

Acknowledgements

Living to be 90 years old can only be to God's glory and credit. His mercy has given me strength when I was weak, and vision when I lost my own. These stories would not have been possible without the faith that has gotten me through my journey.

I thank God that He led me to my husband, Dutch, who gave me nine gems in my crown. Each jewel is blessed with their names, Fred, Sam, Rod, James, Linda, Del, Dwayne, Lauren and Walter, and every one of them are treasures.

When I thought it would be impossible to have a second chance at love, God replaced my sorrow over the loss of my 1st husband and replaced it with my second, Felix Hanley.

Thank you to Fred, who read each chapter's scripture and whose voice will surely give you strength, in the audible version of this book.

A dedicated thank you to sons Fred, James, Del and Dwayne, who read scripture to me daily, have prepared my meals, or driven me to appointments. Being unsighted would have left me at the mercy of many other alternatives I am grateful to have not endured.

A special thank you to Linda, who co-wrote this book, and whose research and patience coaxed my memory and inspired stories.

And finally, to my children, their children, and future generations. This book has been given to you so you that you might know where you come from and realize you are stronger than any challenge you will be faced with in your lifetime. I wondered if that was true when my mom told me this, and when her parents told her the same thing. But they came to the USA to pursue their dream of freedom to believe and realize their God-given purpose. I pray your struggle never leads to leaving a country for the unknown. But if it does, the path has been carved with generations of examples to help you through.

All my love and joy,
Mom/Gram/GG

Contents

Introduction

According to my mother, "Some people don't need an introduction," she says. But if you have ever worried about how to find the love of your life, lost it, lost it all and had to start over, stressed out about how you are going to make ends meet, suffered a great loss, lost a loved one, had a child or nine, stayed up for nights walking the floor sick with worry over them, had to live with setbacks or handicaps, or just plain wondered how you were going to navigate one more of life's curve balls, then you've got to meet my mother, Lorraine Snider-Hanley. Endurance isn't about what you get through, it is how you get through it. And for her, it is her unwavering faith and belief in Jesus Christ that has taken her on this long 90-year journey called life! Each chapter can stand alone in case you are short on time, or we get back to waiting rooms after COVID lets us return to a new normal. It can also be consumed all at once if you want, because each chapter reveals stories of faith, unexpected favor and fulfillment you might not be able to get enough of.

Some people instinctively know what to do in an emergency, while others train for it. But there is no handbook on how to handle stress, love, challenge, sickness, marriage, relationships, work and child-bearing all at the same time, until now!

Raised as the second child of immigrant parents, who brought a rich cultural heritage that included core values of a strong work ethic, take nothing for granted, God first, family second, music and education. But it wasn't always easy. Their parents, my great grandparents saw America as an alternative to persecution for their religious beliefs. Their story could be told just as easily today as it was at the end of the 300-year Romanov dynasty, leading to socialism and

1

eventually communism in Russia, in the late 1890's. Today, as back then, America meant opportunity where none existed there. They packed only what they could carry to meet their fate, under the protection of the night sky, and started their perilous journey with their small children. Kids love a good adventure, until it isn't fun anymore. But read about their daring escape and place yourself in that same boat and ask yourself, "Could I do that?"

Their same strong values brought value with them, tilling the soil of undeveloped North Dakota, with the skills honed for generations as farmers. Even my mom did not escape small farm chores. My brothers and I used to snort at her stories of milking cows, churning butter, or pulling weeds in the garden, with rolled eyes, but only if she wasn't looking at us, of course! Don't think for a second that those ethics were not passed onto my siblings and me. Morning chores, go to school, come home more chores. But you cannot raise a family of nine children with one person doing everything. Everyone must do their part. There was no sitting in the boat without an oar. Everyone rowed.

If my great grandparents on both my maternal sides of the family, that came roughly from the same geographical area and about the same period, had not gained the favor of the political winds of the time, my mother may not have been born in this great country, a land that she loves. Her ancestors were encumbered with getting necessary paperwork, paying as they went, expecting no favors, even being held back in England while a pandemic of measles broke out worldwide. And maybe they didn't have the restrictions seen today, that are trying to slow the floodgates of immigration down, not just by the United States but worldwide. Whatever it took, they fulfilled obligations to get and stay here. I am grateful for this.

A recent but memorable interview I watched of Nicole Avant, daughter of Clarence Avant, the "Black Godfather", Chairman of Motown Records, and 2021 inductee into the Rock and Roll Hall of Fame, spoke about the current immigration crisis. And it is worth mentioning here. She said, "America is the most divine experiment. A nation of yes has built a country that accepted immigrants with open arms at times, and with arms, at others." We watch daily, as television, radio and internet broadcast news about Central Americans and Haitian's trying to cross the southern borders of the United States, Dreamers dreaming of citizenship, or the Afghan's whisked out of harm's way, while others were left behind. Our divine experiment is tested of its mettle and what we stand for as a country.

There has to be a lot more than political reasons that someone would embrace the difficulty of leaving their home and never returning, not looking back. That would take unbelievable faith and belief that what you are going to is greater than what you are leaving, no matter how risky or dangerous it is. Even if it means certain death if caught, or death in the journey

The journey cannot be arduous, difficult, tortuous, miserable, or unhappy all the time. There has to moments of respite, reprieve from the dreary reality of life itself. Having a sense of humor is a must. Some situations we find ourselves in may not be funny at the time but in retrospect we gain insight to the lesson in the journey. And raising the family of nine children, bearing them all in an 81-month period over a thirteen-year span, is a book unto itself. Each child, different in their own unique nature, commanded my mother's combined management skills of a Field Marshall and Lucille Ball. it helped to have a sense of humor, and "the look." Everyone knows the raised eyebrow or downcast eyes 'look'. Humor can also provide the much-needed distraction of taking things too seriously.

Not long ago I was talking to my mom about some of these stories and I said, "Mom! You're getting up there in age, and we won't always have you to give us the oral history," a common method of historical preservation. She said it would take too long. But undaunted, I said, "Nah... we can do this in 30 days." Ha! But it started our journey to capture her life in these stories and preserve her legacy. This gift of love has taken the past 18 months! It is not lost on me that she turned 90 in the middle of this! When she was 87, she realized that after a long fight to save her vision, she had lost it. Therefore, her voice, in this book, is my voice in this writing. In the process I came to know about the love story of her and my father, who passed away in 1975 at the age of 53, way too early. And although there has been a lot of living since then, her stories of overcoming are an inspiration that delivers the promise to the reader of assurance that they are not alone in their struggles or journey.

We often think, "Nobody knows the trouble I've seen." I assure you that if you live long enough, you will! Hers are not boo-hoo stories seeking sympathy because she triumphs through it all. There is no triumph over death and the loss of parents, husbands and even children, as untimely as it appears, because it did not escape her. The only way out is through. And the sorrow and sadness, like the joys and gladness, are points of praise, honor and glory to the God she serves. Joy comes in the morning.

I would be remiss to not offer you a glimpse of the author herself. In a series of interviews done before publishing this book, as an interviewer, I introduce many people to this remarkable human being I call Mom. You can find these stories on her YouTube channel, "Miracles in Faith". Can you believe she has a YouTube channel? She also has a Facebook page, "Miracles on My Doorstep," and even a Facebook group, "Miracles in Everyday Life." Instagram and even IGTV sports her interviews. The recording of the book favors some of the music she wrote and talks to the unsighted community she also volunteers her services in. COVID has not slowed her down. But life eventually will.

Her story is a journey of faith, full assurance, and unexpected favor, as each chapter reveals her unwavering strength and belief in God. Her children, grandchildren and already great grandchildren know her strength. And that strength, through her ministry, will continue to serve as a reminder, not only to my own generation, and their generation but the generations that will follow. God will take care of us.

Facebook Page:
www.facebook.com/MiraclesOnMyDoorstep

Instagram Page:
www.instagram.com/miraclesonmydoorstep

YouTube Channel:
www.youtube.com/channel/UCMvxUPj7wLudV-Y37o-yB4Q

Facebook	Instagram	YouTube
Like & Follow	Follow Us	Subscribe

Blind Faith

*For I know the thoughts that I think
toward you, saith the Lord, thoughts of
peace, and not of evil, to give you an
expected end.*

Jeremiah 29:11 (KJV)

Chapter 1

Blind Faith

If you have ever moved, you know there is a lot more to it than just calling a mover. What goes, what gets donated or even tossed. How many packing boxes, tape and wardrobe boxes would you need? You may wonder if you will be accepted or if it will even work out. Even if you had the option to go back, start all over without losing anything, would you be the same?

But If you had no choice but to go forward, you would approach it differently – like it had to work. Right? You would be determined to make it work. And whether you succeeded or not, you would never forget the experience or challenges you had to overcome. Where would you get the strength to leave the past and leap in the unknown future?

My family had to make this choice. There were no moving vans, telephones, cars, convenience stores, indoor plumbing, hotels, maps, tour guides, a bed to sleep in or a good book to read. What they had was terror. The idea that staying put and accepting the status quo of late 19th century Russia meant certain death. Whether or not they would make it to where they were going, or if they would make it after they arrived did not get a second thought. Like the Israelites, flight was immediate when the opportunity came.

The burning desire to immigrate would have to be so great that despite the challenges of getting to a foreign country, where you do not know anyone or even speak the language, you would still go. Would you be afraid or think it was an exciting adventure? What would it depend on? Your age, circumstances under which you left and the sense of adventure, fear, or a combination of all of the above?

My ancestors were Russian peasants that had the good fortune to become landowners under Alexander II, just a few decades earlier, that required them to repay a 40-year bond to the monarch who had issued this to the land barons, from whom the land had been taken. Before owning land, they were serfs and owned by the government. Owning land must have seemed like winning the lottery today because it changed their fate. Bonds were passed to the next generation of landowners until paid. They were still required to put in their time to maintain the Landlord's parcels.

Autocracy did not allow room for monetary gain. After the mere 11.5 hours working, required to repay the government, families eked out small profits in whatever yields that were not taken. Plots of land were rotated in ownership and were not the best carved out pieces of the landlord's massive parcels. Everyone was equal, except the government. Political unrest was abundant.

My dad, Isaiah Samuel, was born to Kosmo and Mora (Mary in the United States), Harchanko in Kiev, Ukraine, which was still part of Russia. He had three brothers, Alec, Joe and John, and five sisters, Kate, Alice, Mary, Lillian and Anne. Kosmo, an efficient but simple farmer beholden to the Czarist government for the 40-year debt for the land inherited, paid it off early, within a few decades. After giving the requisite 50% annual wheat yield from their fields to the State's government, and frugal use of the remaining yield they were able to sell, they owned this small parcel of land outright as well as a few other peasant's parcels that had defaulted or given up.

As Nicholas II ascended the throne, Russia began introducing a series of reforms including civil liberties, literacy programs, state representation and other initiatives, in an attempt to modernize the empire's 300-hundred-year-old infrastructure. Eventually progress was undermined by Nicolas's own commitment to his one country, one religion, and one autocratic rule.

The family would come to know the true price of religious and political freedom. The foretelling of the ensuing Bolshevik upheaval was on the horizon as everyday became more perilous to even speak of their beliefs. They began to witness their own family's religious freedoms dwindle through persecution, as family members disappeared into labor camps.

This fervent environment meant instability and uncertainty, politically, but more specifically religiously, that could lead to death, as the monarch could attest.

As a young girl, I remember my dad talking about the loss of freedom and how their religious practices were kept secret by hiding their cellar studies with like-minded Shtetl (townsfolk) and praying together. Mora practiced Judaism and was in constant fear of being discovered by military forces. The Czar demanded allegiance to one country, one Russian people, one Russian language and one Russian Orthodox religion. The Czar's government wiped out public religious practices and other sacrifices. Parts of Torah scrolls were torn, memorized and recited. Their stories were recalled and confirmed in letters exchanged with my elder members of the family, who sought to preserve their oral history told to them by their elders.

Opposition to the government grew steadily, led by Vladimir Lenin. The intense and embattled opinions gave rise to the Bolsheviks, the majority faction of the Russian Social Democratic Party. Within a few years, socialism became their platform. The monarch's fight was eventually lost in the bloody streets of Moscow to the 1917 Bolshevik Revolution, ending Romanov's 300-year dynasty and rule. After the socialist Russian Social Democratic Party seized power, they renamed themselves the Communist Party.

Prior to this, the turmoil, uncertainty and pogroms my family endured led to the conclusion that while land ownership was new to their generation, the price it sold for may buy them something more valuable. Freedom. Freedom to think out loud. Freedom to worship in the way they wanted.

Realizing the atrocities that would befall their village by leaving, these ancestors knew they would never see their families or Russia again. The memories of some of them leaving their own parents and grandparents would be a burden that would be unspeakable in the ensuing years. Only a few letters and their stories told to their children remain of the Harchanko family's Russian origins. Longevity ensured the elders, children at the time, would live to tell their story.

Imagine secretly stealing away in the dark of night. It was late 1895, just after the harvest. Fearing the government's forced compliance, they had to move swiftly. Using darkness to carry out their covert operation, and taking only what they could carry, they boarded a waiting boat at the river's edge.

Did they walk the two miles to the market shetle town of Boyarka, a small town with a large Jewish population? Boyarka is located on the Gniloy Tikich River, leading them to the Black Sea. They would use the forest as cover to reach the boat, joining other villagers awaiting their shared fate.

As they navigate swiftly down the river their heads are swimming at the thought of the ones left behind. "What will happen to them? Will they be okay? Will we ever see them again?" as they fixed their sight and looked forward to what the rest of the journey would be like. After hours of traveling, but still dark, they are delivered to the shore of the Black Sea. It is known as a rough sea with winds blowing in from Russia whipping up waves several meters high. You have all that you brought, and your imagination.

Leaving home under these conditions might have been terrifying like the journey of Moses, as he commands and parts the sea to open. Relying on his faith in God, he raises his staff, ordering his people to cross before Pharaoh's soldiers reach them. That faith had to be strong enough to overcome the fear of his people – to follow him at their peril and risk of being swallowed by the waters or being torn apart by the point of the soldier's sword. That faith would likely be matched by terror.

Taking only what they could carry, they fled Russia in search of a home that would give them freedom. Freedom to believe, freedom to worship as they believed.

Arriving in England, they were quarantined, while an outbreak of measles circled the globe. They may have wondered if they would even make it to America. Would they have to stay, or be turned back? They did not look back. They adopted a mindset about looking at the past: I'm moving forward.

A few years later, from the same area, my mother's grandfather, Daniel Bokovoy and his wife, Sophy sought their fate in the same brazen way.

Confirming stories from my dad's family are consistent with the stories of the Bokovoy's. Being discovered studying or meeting in basements led to some of the villagers being detained or imprisoned. Stories came back to the village of incarceration. Imprisonment meant being shipped off to Siberia and never seen again.

Looking over some of the papers of my father's parent's Declaration for Citizenship at Ellis Island in 1895, confirms their desire for this freedom. When the form asked why they sought asylum in the United States, they declared "Persecution of Beliefs." That brief statement says it all.

Pilgrims of the Prairies formally charts the Bokovoy clan from their Ukraine passage to their immigration and travel to North Dakota and provides a history of my mother's family. The book, compiled by several families searching the origins of their families, could have been easily and literally wiped out. The families routinely chose to erase the memories of their former homeland they fled as they eagerly sought America's freedom.

A local Rabbi contacted my grandfather, Jacob and his brother Cornelius, advising them of an open passage on a ship that would leave immediately to England and eventually to the United States. They raced home to tell their father, Daniel, and mother, Sophy.

Helping them secure a buyer for their assembled plots of land, the Rabbi found a buyer and wrote a letter of sponsorship that would enable them to gain meager passage in steerage. Although they retained a small parcel for the family that remained, they were able to acquire roughly the equivalent of $1,500 to gain passage and re-establish themselves in the new country. The Rabbi told them to head to Ellis Island, New York.

My mom's parents, Jacob and Anastasia Bokovoy joined them and the roughly forty other family members and villagers in their passage to America.

Learning another language, culture and surely the difficult passage with the meager provisions of less than third-class steerage had to be difficult for them. They came to Ellis Island with the dream of freedom. That dream fueled the hardships they would face and overcome in the ensuing years. True grit and determination are the hallmarks of my family.

The Harchankos briefly migrated from New York to Pennsylvania and the Bokovoys briefly migrated from New York to New Jersey. Both discovered that land grants were being given by the United States government in exchange for occupying and fencing a rural part of the United States. The government was giving 25% of a section of land. A section is 640 acres, or a square mile. So, homesteading to North Dakota meant they would receive 160 acres provided they lived on it, built one dwelling, and established a perimeter fence within five years. Welcome to America, here is some "free" land.

As they journeyed towards their destination, the train took them to South Dakota where they stayed with previous village neighbors who had previously immigrated to the United States. As the Bokovoy family moved on to North Dakota they left the relationships they had been comforted by on their initial arrival in South Dakota that first winter.

They would not have survived the first winter in North Dakota in their covered wagons to Kief, North Dakota, so families pulled together. They named the town for the Russian village they came from. Children were employed to help. Speed to dig out of the hillsides was their salvation the first winter there. Before the second winter they sought the help of the strangers that had befriended them in South Dakota, where trees were abundant. The lumber needed to continue to build their homes before the second winter was given to them with the provision that this would be paid off later. Credit was born. The kindness of strangers became the commerce of the day. Trees were also needed to secure the perimeter of their homestead, a government condition to ownership, and of course Kief Baptist Church, which was built first.

They built their sod house, dug into the hillside before the second winter. Trust and belief by extended credit, with their word it would be paid back, was how they started their new life in America.

Several years of working the homestead, living in the sod one room house with maybe one window, a set of grandparents, parents and seven children eventually took its toll. When the opportunity became available, Jacob acquired free land available in Canada under Canada's homestead rules, settling in a Canadian border town of Cando that they could access by rail.

The minister of my church, Dr David Jeremiah, spoke on 2/20/2020 and gave a sermon called "Looking Forward." He used a metaphor that is as true today as it may have been the night my ancestor's took flight on their midnight run. He said the windshield of our car is very wide so we can see what is ahead. It helps gain perspective of our situation to look for and see all that is ahead of us. In contrast the rearview mirror is smaller. We can see what is behind us, but it is for reference, a view that is not meant to be our focus. The problem with looking at the past is you cannot see what is coming.

And so, it was with my ancestors. Just one look back. Any delay in their decision or lack of commitment would cost them their lives. Genesis 19: 15-26 tells what happens to Lot's wife when she is the only one to look back as Sodom and Gomorrah were destroyed. Her heart was still with the city she was leaving behind, and she became a pillar of salt.

They swiftly moved forward. They had to have the faith of Noah, who built an ark when there had never been any evidence of rain. He endured the ridicule of his peers, but he kept his heart open to God and obeyed. My ancestors prayed and had committed their faith that God would protect them in their journey.

When we look back, we can be overcome by moroseness, remorse or fear. It can make us not trust and lose our nerve. It also blocks our connection to our faith that God has a better plan than we can come up with.

As I look in the small rearview mirror of my own life, I could not have dreamt of living to be 90 years old, moving from North Dakota to the then-far-away-from-home place like California, have nine children, lose two husbands, endure the death of three children or even going blind before writing this book.

We are all born with a deep longing for something greater than we are. For me, that desire became an awareness that I was lacking something, an understanding that could only be filled by God through his Son, Jesus Christ. For the believer that is when we allow the presence of God to dwell within us, who leaves the Holy Spirit to enter us, and forgiveness of our sins becomes our relief of belief. The belief that God is real is not where belief stops. A lifelong journey requires the daily faith that every breath is a measured gift from God. And

14

commitment. My personal commitment affirms that with man, all things are impossible, but with God, all things are possible (Matthew 19:26 NIV). If you knew or could see the blueprint of your life, would you still commit to it?

This has been my journey. Belief, faith, and commitment have helped me overcome the challenges that life gave me. It encouraged me in the good times and comforted me though despair, loneliness, and fear.

Would I like to see again? Of course, but I do not regret being able to see today. I have enjoyed seeing sunrises, my children's faces, seeing grandchildren become adults and the beauty of the earth through the eyes that painted it onto canvas. I see differently than how my eyes previously delivered vision.

The real site is my faith in God. I have faith and hope to get me through the day. Blindness may be a condition, but blindness of the soul is a choice. Because of my deep faith and belief, I can see. I am moving forward.

We Can Do, Cando

I can do all things through
Christ who strengthens me.

Philippians 4:13 (NKJV)

Chapter 2

We Can Do, Cando

Where in the world is Cando, you ask? It is in the Canadian province of Saskatchewan in a suburb of Saskatoon. By car, it is about 35 miles north of Devil's Lake, North Dakota, which is where my earliest years began, after my parents moved when I was two. Cando is where my mother's father, Jacob Bokovoy, brought Isahiah Samuel Harchanko home for dinner. Sam worked in the local grain elevator. Back then Cando was described as a little hamlet. Not much has changed since the population today is still only 68. Saskatoon is where Jacob met Sam and thought of his young unmarried daughters coming of age.

Sam's years as a bachelor would soon be over. At 36, he was introduced to Jacob's daughters, Anne, 21; Sophia, 19, and Helen, 17. My mother, Sophia, recalled her father coming home excitedly saying that he met a young man that not only spoke fluent "Russian" (most likely Ukrainian), but could also read, write, and speak English like a native!

My grandparents, Jacob "Jack" and Anastasia married their second daughter, Sophia, to Sam on December 25, 1922.

My grandparents had been married since May 1895, shortly after Jacob was released from his 3-year forced "tour of duty" alongside the Cossacks and served in the Russian Army. Their immigration to the United States, then on to Kief, North Dakota in 1899, left them with the scarred memories of their family members left behind. My mother recalled when aunts, uncles or other village members who immigrated with them, the children were sent outside when a discussion began

17

about the *old country*. They feared someone would overhear them and they would lose their freedom.

This is a tradition my mother, now Sophie, carried forward the rest of her life. In 1981 when my daughter Linda and I visited her in Arizona, Linda asked why she did not teach her own children her native tongue, Ukrainian. My mother's answer was swift and curt. "Because when we come to America, we speak English. "

That was that.

Jacob spoke some English and "Baba", my grandmother, spoke none. She would have spoken Ukrainian in the home with her children. Her memory, which was long in years, refused to go past a traumatic incident associated with an invasion of their village. That period, which led them to flee their own homeland, was a result of severe religious persecution. The fact that only four of their fourteen children born to Trofim and Martha Bokovoy survived to adulthood, confirms the horrific slaughter that took place, briefly mentioned in *The Five Brothers of Herchenko*, a family member's collection of written memories.

Sam and Sophie began married life in 1922. They stayed in Saskatoon, Saskatchewan for the first eleven years of their marriage, staying with relatives in Minot on occasion, until they moved to Devil's Lake, North Dakota, in 1933.

My earliest recollection of my childhood, now that I look back on it, is probably when I was 4 or 5 years old at Devil's Lake. Mother was a hard worker and very entrepreneurial. My parents had rented a large house for our growing family, and before AIRBNB ever existed, they rented out the extra rooms for fifty cents a night to conductors and brakemen who traveled the rails, one dollar if it included a meal. My mother also worked at the *creamery* with the unsavory task of defeathering chickens.

Separately they rented a piece of land near their rented house, where my parents planted and grew a large garden during the summer. My dad managed the adjacent vegetable stand that became immensely popular. We rarely took any vegetables home at the end of the day, attesting to my parents' superior talents in the garden. Growing mostly potatoes, tomatoes, carrots, and cucumbers, Devil's Lake was a destination location that brought many visitors that became customers during the summer.

During the winter, my dad rented a counter at the Odd Fellows Lodge, where he was a member. There he sold burgers, soups, chili, and whatever the trend of the day was. This was seasonal work and the Odd Fellow's Lodge was only open until 2 pm, leaving him time to do other jobs, like running a full-service gas station, short lived, despite its destination location, due to the Great Depression.

Driving a car back then was dangerous, even disastrous. You could not go far without needing oil, water or even tires that frequently flattened. Radial tires were not mainstream accepted until the 1970s. This also meant you did not go anywhere without carrying a patch kit or two, with extra glue, a tire pump, and a good jack for the tires. Tires had an inner tube – like a bicycle. And like a bike, the air in the tire meant a better ride. Roads were not the highly engineered highways of today. This meant wear on these tires was largely uneven. If you hit a rut or a divot in the road, you might as well pull over, because the tire was going to go flat. Pulling into a gas station was a necessity that meant service and attention to all these hidden dangers.

Back then there was no self-serve at the pump, which did not catch on until the 1974 gas shortage. California gas prices were made cheaper if you pumped it yourself, but only on the odd or even day that correlated with the last number on your license plate!

Customer service was an opportunity to upsell services at the station. Oil and water were checked, windows washed, and air was checked in all the tires. You might refill the water with the extra gallon containers you carried. When service was good, you gave a tip. That service eventually evaporated by the late 1970s, putting young students and men out of a job. That is called progress.

Back then, the customer got out and stretched their legs, used the facilities, but you could not get a "Big Gulp" or a hot dog. Convenience stores did not exist.

You could see just how much fuel was purchased because the large glass cylinder that was hooked up to the pump was visible to the purchaser. A hand crank had to be cranked side to side to pull the gas up to the glass cylinder that held a max of 5 gallons into the cylinder at a time. Most customers could only afford a gallon. But I watched in fascination as their 5-gallon purchase was siphoned through this glass bubble top to fill the car's tank, which was not often. The large glass cylinder reduced its contents through the pump below as it gurgled and fed the thirsty car tank.

Because we were in the middle of the Great Depression, money was hard to come by for most of the country. If it were not for Devil's Lake being, and still is a destination location, cars would not have frequented my dad's station. That said, there was never a rush of more than one car at a time. Occasionally a car needed an oil change. My 5'4" dad would wave them over a dugout pit, where he released the oil contents directly into the ground. This was saved, then recycled to put on areas where dust might come up.

Before you get indignant, remember there were no environmental hazards acknowledged in the United States at that time. In fact, it was not until December 1970 that the Environmental Protection Agency was even established. Up until then, all dirt roads were routinely sprayed by large trucks with sprayers on the back, spraying oil directly on the road to reduce the dust!

I often raced my sister to tell our dad it was time for dinner because it meant maybe a bottle of orange NeHi, or a penny to put in the numerous candy vending machines he owned. We fought over who would go with him to fill these vending machines he had everywhere a working establishment let him put them.

In early 1936 the country was still reeling from the economic downturn of the 1929 crash that caused the Great Depression, lasting until 1939.

I remember my dad's Model T Ford that he drove to the reservation, Fort Totten, which today stands as the best-preserved military post of the frontier era. It was originally built in the mid-1850s as one of the numerous posts built to protect the overland route.

Although the fort continued to serve as a military post, most of its functions had been replaced primarily by management of Indian affairs over the next decade, after the last building was put in place. By 1890 the fort was decommissioned, and in 1891 became the property of the Bureau of Indian Affairs.

Early settlements in and around Devil's Lake were homesteaded. If the homestead was near a source of water, there was a general prerequisite of planting trees, which were, and remain, a sparse North Dakota resource.

The primary source of income around Fort Totten was an outgrowth of this homestead requisite. When the Native Americans of the Sioux tribe occupied Fort Totten, they thinned cottonwood, and other indigenous trees, preparing them for market to be sold as fuel or to make fence posts to fulfill the other homesteader's requirements to fence their parcels. My dad bought them for a penny apiece, took them back to the house to debark them, and prepped them for the fence posts by chipping away with an ax on one end to make a point, and creating a blunt end on the other. He sold them for ten cents each, after he sold each pile, he returned to collect another 200 that fit into the back of his truck.

When President Franklin Roosevelt traveled through North Dakota in 1936, on a presidential tour, he stopped at a train station near Devil's

Lake. There, my dad hoisted me onto his shoulders so I could see him. Everyone wanted to re-elect him. My dad was so impressed that a man with polio could stand and wave, and smiled at the crowd. Unbeknown to us, the president's son, James, would steady him to a standing position. No one knew he was disabled, let alone crippled from his polio. He gave us hope that this awful depression would be over, and the country would recover. His recovery plan included the WPA (the Work Progress Administration), which began in 1935, and would continue until it was renamed Work Projects Administration in 1939. When this brought $15-90 a month to millions of workers it also brought them hope.

The Free Bethel Church was our home church. Covered by yellowish green mud, with its three steps to get in, we participated in the congregation's activities and did not dare come unprepared – which meant my older sister, Edna, and I memorized a lot of biblical passages.

What I especially remember about my childhood is how sick I was. Being born at 7-1/2 months I weighed under 4 pounds. Time has certainly made up for this, but as a preemie my survival was the first miracle I experienced. My mother suffered three infant mortalities before my older sister was born, and a miscarriage before me. My frail size, weak lungs, and topical skin problems would plague me throughout my life starting in early childhood. That did not stop me from enjoying simple things like tap dance and piano lessons. When my mother's sister, Helen came to visit, she taught me how to embroider.

When I was five my parents bought me a dog, whom I named Sandy. If I had an ice cream, I took a lick, then Sandy did. I loved that dog. Sandy and I would wait for the ice man to arrive once a week with his big block of ice. With a big ice tong, he carried our block into the house and put it in our ice box – early refrigeration. Sandy and I could not wait to get the ice chips that would fall as he chipped away at our block portion. Sandy got her own chip and I got mine, a cure to a hot humid day.

Although it was available, my parents refused *relief* we know today as welfare, food stamps and other government benefits. Even though this would have given the family food and other provisions, my family did not want to be seen taking this. What would others think of them, who watched who got it and talked about it, about their own ability to provide enough to survive on. The ethics my parents were raised with were passed down to every generation since.

The Great Depression brought awareness of the have and have nots. Children do not know they are poor until they realize they are, by comparison. If you grew up in a community of sameness, being poor was hard to detect, because there was not a significant difference between households. Everyone was poor by today's standards.

Our immigrant community did not notice our own accents, but we could sure tell the difference of where another family came from, even if they spoke English. Our Ukrainian community could quickly identify a Polish accent from a Swedish accent, because it was so odd to our ears! Church was interesting since we sang in *tongues*. The elders sat in the back, and the kids in the front. The back pews sang in their native language from a Russian hymnbook. Some sang in Russian, some Polish, some Ukrainian. The kids sang in English.

My two brothers, Ted born in October 1936, and James in June 1938, must have seemed like a miracle to my mom. With so many attempts to have a boy, my little brother Ted became the "only child" for the rest of his life. Momma loved doting on him throughout his life, which suited his personality, which he came to depend on. My other brother Jim was compliant, and went along with Momma's requests, which were few. My older sister Edna, was usually busy reading or practicing piano, leaving me time to play with my little brothers when I was not in school or practicing piano.

As the family grew my parents continued to find other businesses to bring extra income. They were never afraid of hard work, which they demonstrated repeatedly.

After applying for a job as an elevator manager for a grain silo job, my dad got a call from Cargill in Minneapolis. They offered him a job and my dad went to work for them in the tiny town of Max, North Dakota, about 136 miles south of Devil's Lake. He would come home once a month so Edna could finish grade school through the 6th grade. In May that year, the family moved to a small farm, two miles outside of Max, North Dakota, close to the railroad that was next to the grain elevator my dad worked.

The first thing my dad did was install a water storage tank which looked like a giant root beer barrel turned on its side, sitting on a raised double-legged stand, with a spigot. The water was not potable and was strictly used for cleaning up. For our running water, we literally ran after it. We carried our 3-gallon pails down to a well, attached each pail, and dropped it into the water below, reeling it back up by cranking the rope up, then carrying it a short distance back to the house.

Our modern wood stove had to heat the house as well as cook on the stove top, earning its name, stove wood range. I helped chop the kindling and brought it back up to the house. There was a warming oven above the stove, to keep cooked food warm for dinner while you cooked other things on the range. It also had a water reservoir on the side to heat water for inside use. It held about 3 gallons and was always maintained full. There was a corner behind the stove for a washstand, where you washed up, brushed your teeth, and anything else before your weekly bath. Water was then recycled into a 5-gallon bucket after everyone had used it. Two upright apple boxes held the white enamel wash basin with red trim. We recycled everything that had a second life purpose.

We were still renting the house my dad had rented when he first arrived in Max the year before. We would remain there until our new house was built in town a little over a year later. But we still had a garden. There was never a year without one. My dad had a few farm animals including two cows, chickens, pigs, and a dog left behind by the previous owner, by the time we arrived.

In 1939 turkeys were sold at an outrageous price of $.49/lb. My mother quickly ordered turkeys from the Sears catalogue. They arrived in large cardboard boxes at the post office. Each box held 100 chicks and we took them back to a brooder house, which houses and warms the baby chicks. When they got old enough, another set of chicks replaced them as the older chicks were released to the yard. Turkey meat was a luxury. I remember herding turkeys by putting a bell on the alpha turkey, and it would follow me, causing all the others to follow behind. Taking them out to the fields they would stay there until I brought the alpha turkey back. We only raised them for two years because of the amount of work involved raising them and getting them ready for market.

We ordered chickens the same way we did the turkeys, through the Sears catalog, but they arrived at the train depot. My dad would get a call in his office to come get them before they escaped out of their boxes. We would raise them to about a month old before ordering the next set. We would start readying the chickens for market when we had raised about 100 chickens. Of those 100, only 75 were laying hens who were separated from the rest of the farm. The laying hens, called leghorns, produced about 60 eggs a day and were kept in a smaller area away from the rest of the chickens.

After we milked the cows two times a day, the milk was always run through the separator to separate the milk from the cream. We churned butter once a week from the cream we did not sell, in a 5-gallon crock and paddled it until butter was formed.

Of all the products produced on the farm, we only kept what we could consume in one day because there was no refrigeration. On market days, I recall my mother would get heavy butcher paper that was lined with wax, lay it across the back of where the backseat of her car was taken out of the 1934 Chevrolet, as she laid out the hens that had been butchered that morning for market. Farm to table had an extremely specific meaning. It was farm to table same day service.

When we moved from Devil's Lake to Max, I entered the third grade, and was behind in my reading, writing, and cursive writing. My teacher, Elsie Lynn, made sure I was brought up to speed. She spent time with me during the recesses and after school while she instilled the Palmer Method of writing, learning circles and squiggles that would eventually become an artform on the paper we had to supply ourselves.

When the new house was finally ready, we could not wait to move and were so excited. We had a full farmer's kitchen in the basement that housed a cream separator, double-deep farm sinks, a long working table that had a meat grinder, a woodburning cookstove, running water, a drain in the middle of the floor and storage cabinets. Adjacent to this was the root cellar, accessed by stepping down into it from the basement door. It was a dugout dirt pit basement that maintained a constant and cool temperature year-round. There were pit separators that kept the 3-400 pounds of potatoes separated from the beets or other root vegetables that we filled to last the winter. We also kept vats of sauerkraut, and pickled cucumbers or pickles, strings of sausage, slabs of bacon, and other things that needed to be maintained cool but not frozen for the winter. The canned goods, like preservatives and vegetables, were canned in Mason jars and kept in the fruit cellar, a small room off the basement.

After milking the cows, we poured the fresh milk into the top bowl of the separator, and started cranking, to separate the milk from the cream. Skim milk came out one of the two spouts and cream out of the other. Skim milk was kept for the new-born calves which had to be fed a few months before they could be weaned off their mother's milk and take feed. What was not used, was made into cottage cheese. Cream was used for making butter. We sold most of the cream and received a monthly check. It was taken daily to the train depot a few yards away and put on the farmer's train car for market.

Covered cooling crocks held what cream we did not sell. A portion was kept and allowed to sour. Once a week we took the sour cream and made butter with it, plunge-churning it by hand. Sour cream was a runny thick milk. Churning would eventually thicken it to become butter. From that, the butter was squeezed through cheesecloth and laid out to be salted. The milk squeezed out of the sour cream was buttermilk which was saved for my dad and making biscuits and pancakes. The salted butter was formed into a bowl the size of a big mixing bowl. It was distributed by the amounts needed for a meal and the rest kept in the root cellar.

The family kitchen was on the main floor. We had a Youngstown, PA kitchen sink. It had a large basin and vertical cabinet with a 25-lb flour bin that pulled outward, and a right-sided drain board. The 1939 GE electric stove worked most of the time during the summer, if we did not have thunderstorms that shorted out the electric poles. Most of the winter was spent in the dark, except for kerosene and gas lamps, until the REA, Rural Electrification Administration brought steady electrical power through farmer co-ops. The refrigerator was too small to be especially useful for things other than proportional-use dairy products and Jell-O. We always had Jell-O. We prepared meals to be consumed and rarely had leftovers.

When I was 11, my little sister Donna was born in 1942. She instantly became my little doll whom I dressed up and combed her hair every day. Fortunately, I was old enough not to carry her the way little kids carry their dolls. or she would not have survived childhood or kept her limbs! I adored my baby sister and looked forward to rushing home from school, so I did not miss out on anything she was doing.

I remember taking drives with my parents to Minot, to see Billy Graham Assemblies and marveled at the productions of the day. These were held in high schools and introduced me to the sounds of the pianist, Ted Smith, who toured with Billy Graham over the next 54 years. That was a pivotal moment for me as a musician, as I made up my mind to become as good at improvisation as he was.

From that time on I was the go-to person for everything musical. I was regularly active at school and in the community.

My oldest sister, Edna, left home to teach school in 1945, and I picked up her chores, adding them to my already-full list. My mother was very demanding and particular about the cleaning. I also helped my dad with the barn chores during harvest season and could hardly wait for school to start so I could get out of the chores. Practicing piano, in the warmth of the living room, far away from the chores that could not wait, was a luxury.

November 25, 1948 was Thanksgiving Day and Edna was home from her teaching post in Dunseith, about 125 miles northeast of Max. We had a huge dinner, and watched my dad carve the turkey. We had a lot of food – but looked forward to the custard Momma had made that morning, and all the pies.

The following day my mother offered to drive Edna back to her teaching post. They left early and my mom said she would be back by 5. "Do your chores," she said as she left. About 3 pm my dad came home from work and told me not to worry about milking the cows as he would finish this. After waiting for him to come home, I went to check on him at the grain elevator around 5pm. I called out to him and he did not respond. When I could not find him, I went in the grain elevator, but he was not there. I found him on the floor laying in a grain bin below the grain elevator. Without safety guards on the big 6-foot belts, the cuff of his jacket was caught, instantly picking him up and throwing him a few feet down with such force his neck was broken instantly. With the machinery still working I yelled out to him over and over. In an instant he was gone. I went into my dad's office and used the only phone we had, calling central, the central operator. Conveying what had just happened, I asked her to call my Uncle Alec, my dad's oldest brother, who lived in Minot. By the time I ran back to the house, my dad's brother, Uncle Joe, was already there. As soon as I told him what happened he ran to the elevator, a two-block equivalent.

As soon as my mom got home about 6:30pm, I wanted to tell her what had happened, but she instantly started asking questions about my chores. Did you milk the cows, did you separate the milk, did you…" Stopping her mid-sentence, I blurted, "Daddy's Dead!" She stopped in her walk to the house and dropped the bag she was carrying and stared hard at me like a judge that had just uttered the last words of a sentence to the convicted. In total disbelief, then denial, then hysteria, I tried to calm her down as my little sister, Donna, began to cry. She was only 5 but seeing her mother in this state upset her and she intuitively knew something was deadly wrong. My brothers who were still out trapping, as they often did after school, were nowhere to be found.

For moments that seemed like hours, time was suspended as I picked up my mom's bag and led her into the house. No words were spoken now. Long sobs had replaced the hysteria and my mind turned to the unfinished chores my dad had promised to finish just hours earlier. I could not think of anything worse that would take me out of my world I considered normal. My normal world was gone, along with my father. When you have an illness or you are at the end of your long life, death is inevitable - even normal. But not my sweet, healthy, and determined father? This was not normal.

My thoughts were interrupted by my Uncle Joe, who had come back from the grain elevator after the coroner arrived. As the sun began to set, he had come to pitch in and help with the farm chores that carried on even in the wake of this tragedy.

With my dad's passing away on the Friday after Thanksgiving, my mother had to go to Minot and make burial arrangements Saturday morning. She may not have wanted to greet the many families who came to bring a meal or ask if they could help in some way, but she did. Cargill sent someone to take my father's place at the elevator. The grain had to be moved constantly to prevent it from getting so hot it sets itself on fire. The numerous conveyor belts that had been running when I came in meant that my father had been getting the grain ready to be poured into the waiting box car that was next to the grain elevator in order to move it to market.

Momma was caught unaware and totally unprepared for what would be the rest of her life, without Sam. She knew little about her husband's entrepreneurial endeavors. For instance, she did not know he collected serialized silver fifty-cent pieces hidden in pipes in the garage, hidden in unexpected places, or that he still had all his candy machines he had at Devil's Lake.

It was a tough time because I was the only one who knew how to access his safe. I had to put all his business papers in the safe nightly, kept in the house away from the grain elevator in case it burned down. When I opened the safe it was empty except for papers, including three stocks and a few land deeds.

"Where's the money! You have to know where it is!" my mother would say repeatedly. This became a chant, then a war cry. She needed to fix problems now. You can imagine how disappointed and frustrated she was. And I was the closest one to her who experienced her frustration daily.

"Surely you know where he put the money." I went to my dad's wallet and the only thing I found was a piece of paper that was folded over so many times I almost missed it. The only thing it said was "r side S win". This must be a treasure map, I thought. As I thought it over, I began to pace where and what I thought he meant. It was not inside so it had to be outside, in the snowbank, outside the garage. I shared this with my mother. When I came home from school the next day my mother had dug up the entire snowbank and dug 4 feet of frozen ground until she came upon his underground vault. By the time I arrived home she had already laid out on the dining room table, what looked like a vault of Mason jars that were filled with his serialized silver coins, which had been wrapped in moisture-resistant tar-waxed paper. She had worked all day digging along the side of the garage until she found the vault, which also contained his cash box. She explained that the land deed was purchased from the school district and "Daddy had work to do and finish before the land would be granted," she said. The land deeds would take her into two counties, some in Ward and some in McClean Counties.

My dad died in November, but it was not until we cleaned out the garage in January, that we came upon another box. It was labeled, "To my dear wife." Inside, it had a much-needed toaster she wanted, and a card that instructed her to go pick up her new baby blue Ford that had been paid for.

Stand For Something (Or Fall For Anything)

Wait patiently for the Lord. Be brave and courageous. Yes, wait patiently for the Lord.

Psalm 27:14 (NLT)

Chapter 3

Stand For Something (Or Fall For Anything)

Not knowing about all my dad's financial affairs was bad enough, but not knowing anything about what he did, let alone how to do it, was doubly hard on my mom on such short notice! My dad must have never wanted to bother her with these things. And that would be a lesson to me early on. She was busy running the farm and field - two full time jobs, while raising five children - but maybe they could have carved out some time to understand the mechanisms of how and where everything was. So, the Good Lord only knows when our expiration date is, because we surely do not.

Very few people plan to have a disaster, but a disaster takes advantage of the unsuspecting, and especially the unprepared.

Compensation from Cargill turned out to be less than $100 a month. This would not even get us through a month. This was an early, but vital, lesson to me I would carry into my adulthood, but it would take a few lessons more for me to understand its importance. Back then I knew, in my 17-year-old mind, that Mom was not ready to take the reins of life by herself. I do not think we can be ready to take those reins when we are dependent on them for our own survival. Double down when we are also taking care of others for their survival. So, a plan is vital.

What we lacked was a plan for the everyday, practical things that get us through the day or month beyond the most immediate needs of the children and the animals and fields that produced market income and the original farm to table we depended on for our own survival.

Mom understood she would have to provide what my dad, Sam had, when her month fell short of providing for all those she took care of. As women do, far too frequently, she was the last on the list for her to provide for.

Aside from personal hygiene, she faced oncoming challenges of a cold winter, tilling the fields, and tending cows, chickens and children like a field marshal in a battlefield. Dependent on discipline and structure I never detected the difference of the cold winters' howling winds from her sobs in the night as she must have lay there wondering, "Why this, why now, and how am I going to get through this."

One thing I can say for sure is that she never whimpered, whined or said, "I did not sign up for this, I quit!" Her parents sacrificed everything to get to America. As did, Sam's parents. Both families had fled the suppression of what became a war-torn battlefield of conflicting political and religious ideologies for the land of the home, the brave and yes, free. Free to worship, free to speak, frcc to be. But what is free when you have no context for that? Her context was sacrifice. And she knew what she had to do to preserve the reason and history of such a daring escape of her and her husband's families just a few decades earlier. So, no matter what her hardship was that she faced, it paled in comparison to the sacrifice her and Sam's parents had made, knowing that the generations left behind would be punished or annihilated and that she would never see them again. Her future was clear. Forge ahead. With her own new plan.

Growing up in a small town outside Minot, North Dakota in the 1940s might be like living out in the country of a small European village in the late 1800s. The limited social life, without a phone, let alone internet, was limited to the few hours we could get broadcasted on the radio, and only after our farm chores were done.

We slowly got through the community's well wishes as we buried my father, and winter set in. As we planned the spring planting and harvest, I thought about what the next school year, my senior year, would look like and how I was going to juggle the school activities, music, and now extra chores that would have been done by my dad. I needed a plan. That meant I had to teach my brothers how exciting these chores were, and how rewarding it would be, and more helpful to our mom. She would plan what to sell, what crops to plant, and what livestock to sell. I would plan how to get them to be excited enough to help! I am not sure whose job was harder!

During late winter, as the winds howled off the plains, we listened to the radio as life resumed, and our new normal settled in. It was the coldest winter I could recall. It was the first time we had to run a thick cable from the back porch to the barn, and tether ourselves to it so we were not lost in the snow drifts, then frozen in the minus 60 below zero weather we were hit with.

On occasion the Farmer's Co-Op sponsored events that encouraged proper socializing that we sometimes heard about on the radio broadcast when we could get it. There were no proms, spring dances or things that might lead to a proper courtship. The Farmer's Co- Op took it upon themselves to create the most natural but recurring annual disaster!

On some occasions these events were *basket socials*. A basket social required a basket brought by a young marrying-age woman to be put up for bid or auction. The basket was then purchased by a hopeful young male suitor attending the event. The clever Co-Op event then required the basket to be shared between the two during that same social function.

The basket was generally put together with great care by the parents of the young participating females. The boxes, or baskets were sort of like a secret Santa in that you did not know what was in the box, except, unfortunately, you could not trade it for something better with someone else. The main purpose was to encourage pairing so the Farmer's Co-Op did everything they could to provide an environment where you could pick a date. There was no Tinder App on a smartphone. It was an actual social event held face to face, and you might have to see that face repeatedly, socially. Even if it was a disaster! Maybe that is why there were so many of these events. They were immensely popular in the winter and the spring, after the crops were planted. *Human harvesting* at its best.

If a young lady did not want a suitor her basket might not be decorated as elaborately as one really seeking the attention or affection of an ardent suitor, because she was responsible for this part of the box. The parents were responsible for what went inside.

These events were only known to the parents for some reason – maybe to avoid a sudden onset of stomach flu or fainting spells from menstrual cramps for those who really did not want to attend. The element of surprise generally netted the largest attendance, as was the case for me.

When I was in my senior year, I had just come in from school and saw a large box on the sideboard. I asked my mother what that was. She said it was for a box social I would be attending. I had no idea what that was. Was it a box of her famous vegetables to be given to someone? But why freshly fried chicken and recently canned dill pickles? I did not know. I only knew that two sisters who were also members of the Co-Op, would be picking me up.

As the bids started, some baskets were sold extremely fast, and the socializing began. Then it was my basket. Bids were quick, but as I watched in horror, someone I did not want to get the basket continued to outbid all the other bidders until he won!

Although I had gotten there with his sisters, who were already happily married and working on their own farms with families of their own, I quickly made the connection that we could all be related in the future. I am not certain if there was "insider trading" information exchanged between his sisters and him, or not, but he seemed to know who owned my basket. Bidding was supposed to be anonymous, but he seemed to be licking his fingers with every bid for that chicken.

It was customary to eat the contents of the basket under the lights, and supervision, of the hall where the auction took place. Larry, not his real name, wanted me to join him in his car! Since there were no behavioral rules for how the contents would be consumed, I followed him to his car. He got behind the wheel and patted the seat, encouraging me to scoot right over next to him. I had repeatedly stammered his name and never looked him in the eye at church, and now, suddenly, we are going to his car alone, away from the rest of the crowd? My heart froze, and apparently so did my feet. I stood my ground outside the car, with the door open as the night breeze chilled me to the bone, hoping to chill any ardent ideas he seemed to have on his mind!

You cannot imagine how many topics from cow milking, what kind of fertilizer his farm was using on certain crops or how interesting I found his short answers were, but I encouraged him to tell me more about each topic! The more he tried to steer conversation towards the moonlight, the more I put a little sunshine on the safe side of conversation, if you know what I mean. I even quoted scripture. That usually has the effect of a cold shower with young men, but he seemed to enjoy the spice of the chicken so much that his peppered comebacks were spoken with fiery repose. At that point, I began to discuss the treatments I was seeking for my skin that was diagnosed as eczema but that just seemed to get him going. He wanted me to show him my worst places affected, which as of this writing, at the age of 90, I still blush at. It was behind my knee, behind my ear and elbows. I certainly was not going to tell him about my armpits. That young man had mating on his mind, and I was not going for it.

Deep inside I also knew I was afraid of him, or maybe me. Although he was two inches shorter than me, and much slighter built, there was something about his demeanor, and taking me away from the social function, that sparked fear in me. I also did not like this situation because I had no idea how to handle his advances he apparently had on his mind. Clearly, I had not thought this all the way through prior to sitting on the passenger side of the front seat, now with a death grip on the door handle. Since I feared he had some desire to get me closer, I was going to do everything I could to avoid and redirect his conversation, his eyes, and especially his hands. In retrospect he would not have qualified as a featherweight, under 120 pounds, but in my mind that farm boy behind the wheel might as well have been Paul Bunyan.

Most young ladies' parents were at the social event and the parental peer pressure most likely prevented mishaps that could occur. However, with my father passing away a year earlier, my grieving widowed mother had her hands full with the farm, children, and animal husbandry, and I was on my own. But if my mother had been there, she would have been in the back seat, making sure this young man enjoyed every single bite of the chicken and dill pickles she prepared for him. And there would have been plenty of light. All the doors would have been opened, if we'd even made it to the car, the interior light, and headlights on high beam – probably so someone would know where to find his body if he had tried something. My mother was tough. I hoped that I would be able to overcome any advance he might make and prayed for strength.

But Mom and Dad were not there. It was him and me. Every young person is going to get challenged. And in your lifetime, you will be challenged repeatedly. It can be moral, legal, or ethical situations you are put in. At 90 I have lost count of how many times I was challenged or asked to compromise my own belief. But it is the moral compass that is within all of us that keeps us steady and able to live with ourselves and our decisions. I have taught my own children that if you do not stand for something, you will fall for anything.

I did not eat a thing, afraid that if our hands touched, he would take a more intimate step towards me. To his credit he did not, because I kept him busy by pointing out all the good things in that basket. There is a lot of truth that a way to a man's heart is through his stomach and I was counting on that until I could get back to the safety of the social hall.

It was in that moment, call it Divine intervention, that I thought I heard someone call my name. Hearing that voice of God, and I was sure it had to Him, I leapt out of the car and encouraged Larry to do the same, as he followed far behind my swift steps back to the hall.

Maybe it was intentional on my mother's part to marry her daughter off. This grieving widow had enough to deal with trying to figure out how to farm the acreage without a husband, and raise three other younger children, that my coming of age must have seemed overwhelming to her.

I was consumed with the itching, irritation and weeping of my skin caused by the eczema, and wheezing caused by my asthma. But I knew one thing that day. I had no interest whatsoever in the *box social dating app*. I was grieving my own father's passing and missing his wisdom in what he might have done. He was not the over-protective type, since his work required him to be at the grain elevators for such long hours, especially during harvest when it was still light at 11Pm. I did not know him in the many ways fathers enjoy shared parenting today, that develop much deeper relationships with their children. But I knew he loved me and had my back. It is odd that I would still find this story in my life as relevant today as it was then. You might get talked into something you later regret but I hope the insight of this young 17-year-old gives you hope and promise that your personal values are strong, and that you have the courage to speak up and not get talked into something you will later regret. More importantly your values will become the very culture and foundation you live your life by.

Take Care Of My Date Please

Humble yourselves, therefore, under God's mighty hand, that he may lift you up in due time. Cast all your anxiety on him because he cares for you.

1 Peter 5:6-7 (NIV)

Chapter 4

Take Care of My Date Please

Immediately after the Box Social, mother realized this event was not going to lead to any future relationships, let alone marriage, for me. And for sure this was not the way I wanted to have a date or meet my future husband. This could not be the only way to find someone to build a life with. At 18, almost 19, however, I was so miserable from my skin condition, likely contributing to my asthma, that dating was the last thing on my mind. Although well-intended, this event left me with further resolve about my mother's hand-picking a suitor for me, and shaken.

After spending years tolerating treatments that irritated my skin more, I wondered if I would ever find an alternative that worked. Seeking my own remedies had to be better than my mom's sulfuric and molasses treatment. Imagine taking something that smelled like burnt matches, or bad eggs, or worse! Assuring me that this treatment would cleanse my blood, Sulphur and molasses was required to be consumed. Not even a spoonful of sugar or whiskey would have dulled the sensation of swallowing this combination. Then to make sure the treatment was a success I had to wash it back with a cup of raw goat milk. I gag thinking about it even today. As I watched my mother mix this concoction I would hide, like a pet trying to avoid a bath... behind the stove, in corners – anywhere to avoid this treatment. Although my mother was convinced of its medicinal and healing powers it was totally ineffective and just plain nasty.

My eczema flare ups were generally caused by some allergy, hormonal intervention, or stressor. Lady Gaga and I had one thing in common – I was born this way. I was handed to my mother in a blanket as a preemie, with splotchy and red skin flaking off my incredibly young body.

Another homegrown treatment for my irritated skin was being wrapped in bandages of pure lanolin. I can honestly say today that I still cannot look a sheep in the face favorably. At first this treatment felt good. But within minutes my skin was so itchy and irritated, it made me insufferably miserable.

In early grade school I never worried about how my skin looked because I did not have to get undressed to play sports. I never swam, so my bad skin secret was safe with me. But when I got into high school, I had to be more deliberate about hiding my breakouts. Outside of the usual pimple or hormonally induced breakout, my skin had a mind of its own. I never knew what I would wake up to and the odd combination of my wardrobe reflected these routine breakouts. Long sleeves and high necks even in spring and fall were standard. Socks were common so that was not a stand-out. I could not risk total community humiliation by showing my elbows, forearms, or even legs – all which was required in a uniform, if I had played a contact sport like girls' basketball. So, I became a master of deception by using my developing talents as a pianist to accompany the men's choir during girl's physical education, so I did not have to suit up.

My favorite treatment was from my mother's medicine cabinet, "Lydia Pinkham's Tonic" which was originally intended to ease symptoms of "the change", we now call menopause and premenstrual cramps. No one talked about these things except in hushed tones. The tonic was intended to help with other ailments generally attributed to any "female disorder".

The tonic was a closely guarded treatment that was mail-ordered from the Fuller Brush salesman that knocked door to door in the day.

Fortunately, my mother only allowed me a 4-ounce treatment 3 times a day for the worst of my flare ups. I say fortunate as I could have easily become a future poster child for Alcoholics Anonymous. This tonic was that good. Shortly after my mother passed, my sisters and I were going through her kitchen and discovered a bottle of this old treatment. Although it did not have the list of ingredients required today, it did mention 40-proof alcohol content on the label. Now come to think of it, this could have been used for many other ailments like insomnia, test results, or a failed driver's test. Just saying.

Mother sought the advice from so many doctors they began to seem like "palm readers" to me. Not one doctor we saw advised her of anything that treated my condition or provided me relief beyond a few hours. The most honest doctor told me to "just live with it" – like I had a choice!

My mother had her hands full with my treatment, four children under the age of 18, and the large farm she now had to single-handedly manage, after my father's death a year earlier.

Call it divine intervention but have you noticed that when you need something desperately and it seems impossible, that God does this seemingly, but amazing, magic trick. I say this sincerely because this has happened so many times to me that coincidence is not even a remote explanation. Whether it is you being awakened by a song in your head that seems to write itself or you see a big sign on a billboard that screams out an obvious (of course only to you) answer, God delivers a message to you. I say obvious because even though it is in plain sight that everyone can see - that specific message is delivered to you, and only you, in the context that you are meant to see and get. It is the answer to your prayers.

Now sometimes we are not listening or even noticing because we are so wrapped up in our thoughts, problems or even misery. God is not deterred. That message has been ignored so many times by the intended recipient, that a billboard is literally required for us to see it! But God never gives up on us despite our ignorance or inability to faithfully see His answers.

This was one of those billboard moments. Clearly a message was being delivered to me in a magazine I was pouring through. Magazines were a luxury and never delivered to our farm, so it had to be in the waiting room of yet another doctor's office seeking another treatment. But that message was as clear to that 18-year-old as it is today. A quarter page ad showed men and women in a mineral water pool claiming treatment for any, and all, bone or skin ailment, headaches, arthritis… all through natural hot spring mineral baths. We did not tear pages out of magazines so others could read it, so I quickly wrote down the address to the mineral springs and scnt a request for brochures. Three weeks later information and the brochures arrived. With loads of testimonials claiming the benefits and delivery of relief sought, this was enough for me to take to my mother.

My mom concurred this might be the treatment needed and agreed to send me by train to Plains, Montana. My suitcase was packed for a month. The farm was still under snow, so it was a logical time for me to go. My breakouts were the worst in the winter – maybe from the contrast of heat and cold, the multiple layers of clothes that always irritated my skin or both. It was March and I was headed to Plains, Montana. Not knowing that Plains was still far from Hot Springs, I encountered a new problem on my arrival, that I was not sure how to fix. I had been sent on this trip with only enough money for the hotel that included meals. Hot Springs was at least 20 miles away and it was lightly snowing. Walking was out of the question. As I sat on my suitcase next to the boarding area, I prayed for a miracle. A mail carrier was at the train station to pick up the mail. As we were talking, coincidentally, she said she was going to Hot Springs to deliver the daily mail. I guess you know we both got into her old but extremely long car.

After checking into the hotel and getting settled in, I went to the hot springs bath. Oh, what a relief! The itching and redness slowly disappeared within a week. Feeling so much better – and my skin looking more normal, gave me a huge emotional and physical lift. So much that I felt like socializing and sought out the fellowship of a local church. I quickly immersed myself into the youth group and began to participate in activities designed for this age group. The more I attended, the more I got involved with the youth in this group. There was always something interesting to do, someone new to meet, and an exciting alternative from all the chores I did not miss back on the farm.

The hotel manager's daughter, Peggy, was part of this youth group. Seeing her frequently at the hotel we had a chance to become friendly. Peggy told me she had invited a young man she had met in town to church that Sunday. She was busy with the choir and would not be able to meet him at the church door. Since my socializing had not led me to join the choir yet, she asked me for a favor. "Take care of my date," she asked.

When I asked how I would know who he was she described him. "Wait for the tall thin man with wavy black hair wearing a plaid green mackinaw (jacket). Tell him I will meet him at the malt shop after church. Will you please sit with him until I get there?" Not having any reason to deny this request I patiently waited at the church door until Dutch arrived. Recognizing him from the description I led him to a pew and sat next to him. After the church service we all went to the malt shop. He sat at the counter with Peggy on one side and me on the other.

As a young woman I was suddenly presented with choices I never had before. Do I want a malt or a shake? Does anyone want to go to a barn dance? Kids just talking. But I was excited about being there and experiencing things that were so new to me. Maybe everyone in that group was used to this but I was a farm girl from North Dakota, and this was just so exciting. A malt, a shake, coming and going as I pleased. I never wanted to go back home. "What's a barn dance," I

45

asked. Realizing I had never been to a dance, Peggy's "date" asked if I would like to go, when he realized that no one else, including Peggy, expressed any interest in going. Was it in a barn? The square dance turned out to be in the school cafeteria and he took a reluctant farm girl onto the dance floor for her very first dance. But I was so self-conscious that I shied away from the dance circle. He asked me what was wrong. I told him I thought everyone was looking at my bad skin and I felt embarrassed. He told me to be myself and stop worrying about what others thought of me. He apparently did not see my flaws, even when he pulled me up from the floor after a spin that sent me swiftly over my two left feet onto the floor. We were both laughing so hard we did not notice the time pass so quickly. His encouragement gave me a sense of peace and well-being. There is no other explanation for self-worth. Why should I worry about what others think? If I believed God accepted me as I am, why wouldn't I believe that a man could too? It was at that moment that I realized that this charming man saw more in me than I saw in myself. Charm, good manners, and kindness allowed me to take a real liking to him.

Soon after, he began accompanying me from the hotel to the spa and back. We talked about my life on the farm and his recent tour of duty in the Navy. He even invited me to his home where I met his parents, brother, and sisters. Meals, walks, and talks followed till we were inseparable.

Money began to run low, but the treatment was really working and giving me a renewed confidence in myself. It did not hurt that an ardent admirer also found me attractive.

Reluctantly, one afternoon, I explained it was time for me to go back home - to North Dakota - and get back to work on the farm. He was silent for a while, and he seemed to be contemplating what I had just said. I could never have been prepared for what he said next. All I can say is that divine intervention and God's hand was on my shoulder. That "Take care of my date" request from Peggy, the second week after my arrival, became a proposal for marriage to Dutch, just five weeks after we had met.

I took care of her date. From that moment on, and for the next twenty-five years in marriage, until his death, we took care of each other.

It Was A Billboard Moment

And we desire that each one of
you show the same diligence so as
to realize the full assurance of
hope, until the end.

Hebrew 6:11 (NASB)

Chapter 5

It was a Billboard Moment

It had been a little over a year after we were married, that I returned to the farm to introduce my husband and our first-born son, Fred, to my mother, brothers, and little sister. After Dutch proposed, we were immediately married in his parents' living room, surrounded by his family in attendance.

Momma was working the farm and would not be able to put the spring crops in the field if she had come. It would be hard enough for her to handle the farm, especially without my help now, and I did not want to burden her.

It was around my birthday in May, and she was elated to hold her first grandson. The visit was brief, and after a week, we headed back to Montana so Dutch could start apprenticing in the plaster trade, a profession he would work for the rest of his life. Each work assignment, roughly a month, took us to another part of Montana.

The sense of adventure began to fade as each move from a furnished bungalow to another furnished bungalow slowly ate away at our profits. The focus was on his work, not mine, because we moved every 4-6 weeks for the next job. The promise of work may have kept us moving - but not moving up. Each job meant he could practice his craft though, which after a year, he was getting fairly good at.

While we were in North Dakota, we met several people in his trade who said they would contact us if there was work. My father- and mother-in- law ran a flower shop in Hot Springs, and we frequently checked in on them. They were the family switchboard, so leaving a message with them was the only means of communication we had. They were our answering services.

When we got word there was work in North Dakota a few months later, we headed back there. This time I would be taking my new son, Sam, with our growing family back to stay briefly with my mother, while Dutch commuted to Minot.

While he commuted about thirty miles between Minot and Max, I stayed and helped my mother in the acres of gardens, along with my siblings and my two sons. I humorously thought about one of the last times I had been home, before I met my husband, and the time my mother tried to play matchmaker, with very little success. It would be another 20 years before my mother and I could talk about that, because our relationship had not yet evolved to be able to talk of such things. And even twenty years later she would still say, "What a good catch he would have been!" But while I worked the garden, I counted myself lucky to find a man who loved me unconditionally, as I continued to pull weeds and harvest vegetables.

Each day Dutch would say he was tired of the commute after a hard day's work. Back then, a thirty-mile commute was unheard of. It was far more common to be home after work within 10 or 15 minutes. The old windowless, green-paneled service wagon required him to drive at a lower rate of speed than he would have liked. It took him an hour each way. In the winter, the commute was even longer.

Even though he and I got along well with my mother, our living situation was less than ideal. Fred and Sam were active and demanded attention. When their dad got home it took a while for everyone to settle in. In any event, he had plenty of time to think about us and his growing family. Maybe he thought about his growing responsibilities, but a long commute meant he was away from his family too long and too much.

The commute was dotted with billboards, some with one-piece bathing suit-clad women with big beach hats, provocatively posed, and smoking a Pall Mall cigarette on a beach; or Brylcreem's "A little Dab'll Do You" men's hair products, and even Burma's Shaving Cream, that promised, over a 5-mile sequence of billboards, separated by a mile between each one, a new and clever message, leading to the final marker, Burma Shave.

A beard (then a mile)

That's rough (then another mile)

And overgrown (now you're trying to figure out the rest of the rhyme)

is better than (you have a mile – and you're laughing at your thoughts)

A chaperone (of course – but at least you've gone 5 miles!)

Burma-Shave

These billboards kept his attention on the long drive back. It was one billboard, in particular, that caught his attention, and he could not wait to come home and tell me. He excitedly talked about the Pierce billboard that advertised new and affordable homes on wheels. At the time, I had never heard of a trailer. It made sense to me - a car could pull something that would trail behind it. We could continue to follow his trade and have some reliable place to call home. Mind you, this was not a double-wide or anything we might see in retro today. But the idea that I could be close to him, and he could eliminate his hour long commute each way, sounded like a dream come due.

That little 28-foot, very well-used trailer, was delivered to the Wigwam Trailer Park in Minot. We could not afford a new mobile home or trailer. We had to make do with what we could afford. It was paid for with money borrowed against my husband's wages. At that time, a good week was $50-75. Today, that would be the equivalent of

$650/week, but costs were low and rent for parking the trailer was only $20 a month and groceries were $20 a week. You could fill your car up for less than $2.00!

As the winter set in, work became scarcer. Work always dried up around the end of the year. We had heard there was work in Fargo, North Dakota for a few months on a commercial building. At that time of year, the coldest part of winter, it would have been extremely dangerous to move the trailer, so it made sense to stay put. Besides, Minot work would start back up in mid-spring.

The Fargo commute was much farther than anything we could have anticipated. It was well over 260 miles each way. This was a little over 5 hours each way at 50 mph, if he was lucky. Dutch would not leave me, the two boys, and a third on the way without a car, so he hitchhiked back and forth from Minot to Fargo. Sometimes he got a ride right away and sometimes it took a few hours. He left on an early Sunday afternoon and hitchhiked back on a Friday after a full day's work, usually not arriving back until early Saturday morning. To say it was less than ideal is an understatement. Frostbite burned his ears in those frozen hours, as he waited for a ride. No matter how many layers of warmth he put on, it was no match for the howling winds causing windchill factors to drive the temperatures down to minus forty degrees.

I worried about him. He worried about me, and the task of taking care of our small children, alone. But neither of us complained. I reached deep for my own faith to pull me through some dark days, remembering that "This too shall pass," not, "This too won't *last*." I believed with all my faith, that God would not give me anything I could not handle. I trusted this faith for my daily strength, which would have to sustain me for over three months.

My husband eagerly checked back to pay the weekly rent, fill the gas tank, and go shopping. Like a bird who does not worry where the morning food will come, I knew that I would be taken care of. We did not speak of the commute as a hardship. And if my husband thought it was, he never said so.

Starting in April that year, work really started picking back up and we were able to put a week's salary away. Spring is one of my favorite times of year. The earth starts to thaw and show signs of hope as plants and flowers spring up to reach for the sun. This also meant I could take the boys to the park, where they could run and jump, or they would pile up in my lap for the swing ride. There was not much room for toys at the trailer park, but the spring sun meant they could ride a small trike on the concrete pad next to the trailer or get in the wagon and be pulled for a ride on my numerous morning errands.

It was the first day of May, and it was greeted with our new baby boy, Rodney. At that time, hospitals kept the newborn and mother in the hospital for five days – probably to get the much-needed rest before going home with a new addition to the family. My mother took care of Fred and Sam and loved having the boys at the farm. She would later tell me tales of the boys and their playing in the garden. There is just something about boys and dirt, that no matter what you give them to play with, will keep them occupied for hours. Fred loved to pick potato bugs. Although he probably did not know the difference between a penny or a nickel, he loved exchanging a bug for a coin with his grandma. Those were happy times.

Weekends meant more family time and occasional outings. Fred and Sam were always ready, and eagerly bound into the car for an adventure. I wrapped my new baby boy in a bundle and bound into the car myself. Sometimes we went on a drive, and sometimes to a park where the boys would each get a popsicle from a vendor and squeal, for what seemed like hours, as their dad pushed them on the merry go round.

Fred took early charge, always helping and asking if he could help. Sam was quiet, and followed Fred like a shadow, and was quite content to just sit with his toys and play on the blanket. The trailer was getting smaller and smaller as each new member of the family was added. Thank goodness the children were small. The two older boys slept in one bed, and Rod in a bassinet. As Rod started to grow, so did his dissatisfaction for not being able to keep up with his older brothers, as he learned to stand up. His frustration was satisfied only when he was able to join the boys on the blanket if we were outside.

The trailer began to resemble a modern-day preschool. The trailer was a small room, had a changing table, and a learning environment based on monkey-see-monkey-do with the boys. They learned so fast from one another. Thankfully, none of them were capricious or tried to get into anything.

With living quarters so small, paying attention was a fulltime job. We did not have child safety locks for the cabinets, cover plates, or safety plugs for the outlets. A gentle hand or redirecting their attention from the things they were naturally curious about was how I spent most of the day.

I loved each one of my children, and the children were secure in this. Over the next several years, as my family continued to grow, it would be this same love that would shield them from unwanted stares, or unkind words from a shopper in a grocery store. When I was asked, "Are they twins?" "Triplets?" I said, "No." these gawkers seemed to want to create a logical explanation, in their minds only, for the size of my family.

Then, like today, many families bring their children to the market – some as an outing. Then, it was a necessity. We did not have babysitters, and the only logical place for those children was to be with me.

I did not always share the feelings I felt with my husband, but it was hurtful to be ridiculed for something so joyful as bringing a child into the world. Maybe their questions were curious, but the looks and rolling eyes or the laughing and condescending tones as they walked off was meant to ridicule me.

Some weekends we would go visit my mother at the farm. There were three of my siblings still at home, and one of my brothers, Jim, would have fun playing with the boys as my little sister, Donna, and Mom and I caught up. Mom always had some treats for the kids. But cookies, Rice Krispy treats, or cakes were accompanied by a tall glass of milk, and always sitting down at her kitchen table. The boys loved to chase the chickens who, thankfully, could run faster than them, or pet the new calves born in the spring. But they would have nothing to do with the geese, who would occasionally chase *them*. Mom had at least a dozen geese and ducks, but they made so much noise that she got rid of them that spring. On a farm you do not get rid of an animal, you *repurpose* it. It was an active farm, and the boys loved running into the enclosed barn, and jumping in the hay, or collecting eggs under the strict supervision of Grandma at the chicken coop. After a full day of fun, everyone was totally exhausted, and they gladly helped us get into the car as they waved their final farewells.

As we drove away, there was a sort of homesickness that comes from knowing your mother will not be fixing your daily meals anymore, or the daily chores of the previous family life would never be the same. I was grateful for the sun that already set, as my eyes welled up with tears. The distraction and responsibility of having my own family helped me ease this separation. To make me feel even better, I was also grateful that the Box Social had not worked out.

I am sure it was with the best of intentions that my mother's call out to God was for her as well as me, to find a suitable husband. God answers our prayers. Sometimes it seems like they may go unanswered because we want a quick fix, or we think we want a particular outcome. But God hears us and delivers His answers according to His will. All things are possible through those who love the Lord.

And while Dutch was not whom my mother picked, she loved him as if she had.

I Prayed for a Miracle

Do not be anxious about anything, but in everything by prayer and pleading with thanksgiving let your requests be made known to God.

Philippians 4:6 (NASB)

Chapter 6

I Prayed for a Miracle

The experience of our third winter together is still with me. The trips to Fargo, North Dakota were hard on my husband. Despite his covering and winter gear clothing, he still got frostbite on his ears. I knew how painful it was for him, and as they started to heal, hurt even more. Minot, North Dakota is a midwestern state, dominated by the Great Plains. With no visible mountains, it is located sixty miles south of the Canadian border. To find a mountain range required a full summer's day drive to either the Canadian Rockies, to the northwest, or equal distance southwest to Montana's West Glacial, the Eastern entrance to Glacier National Park. Today a train can take you between these two points, but bring a book, and a few meals. It still takes twelve hours and seventeen minutes!

With flat plains, the wind had no barrier and would frequently show off its force. The winds would come howling down from the north, bringing heavy snow. Leaving your car for even an hour, say to go to church or school, the wind could create a ten-foot snow drift and you would be snowed in. We often waited for the winds to die down, then scurry to replenish provisions before the winds came back up. Driving in this weather was also treacherous because you could not even see the road. Weather was generally cold, at minus twenty-five degrees, but that winter was especially cold. In January it got down to approximately minus forty degrees, but with the windchill got as low as minus 60 degrees. This was just dangerous. It humbles me to think of the sacrifices my husband made to make sure there was money for rent and food.

That experience in the bitter cold of winter was a gut check for both of us. We had spoken of going to California a few times because, we thought, it just had to be warmer year-round. Not having to shovel snow away from the door just to get out, kept my mind occupied with the boys and how cold this would be for them growing up. I had weathered it, but I thought about this economically. The boys had to be outfitted with special snow jackets, snow boots and snow suits. We had started buying clothes in August for the upcoming winter. Overshoes to go over the snow boots were expensive; head bolt heaters to keep the car's engine from freezing when it was not running, and antifreeze to keep the radiator from freezing, and so on. The middle of November through the middle of April was the winter season. This six-month winter, with getting the boys bundled up to go out was a fulltime job. I kept plenty of flour and yeast on hand, and the boys would frequently wake up to the smell of fresh warm bread. My mother would bring a roast or a chicken every few weeks. This would last us almost two weeks. After the initial feast, there were leftovers, then soup stock and what was left could be boiled off the bone. This was especially good in that tiny trailer. The soup would steam up the room and bring a warmth that was strengthened by the smells coming from that pot and hot fresh bread.

But it was also a reality that my husband did not want to go to California. He had family in Watsonville, California, and his recollection about his stay in California was not memorable. He said it was hot – even humid. He served in the Navy as a medic and was stationed in Northern California from 1942 to 1945. He was stationed at Mare Island and did not want to return. He had ventured down Central California on a few excursions with his Navy pals. Central California is California's single most productive agricultural region and, today, is one of the most productive in the world, providing more than half of the fruits, vegetables, and nuts grown in the United States. But to him, California was no match for the Big Sky Country memories of his youth, that he always looked forward to returning. But I am sure he had second thoughts as he waited out in the cold to hitch a ride to and from Minot to Fargo

It was so cold in that tiny trailer, that keeping it heated from the elements was challenging. We made sure the heating oil, held in a 50-gallon tank adjacent to the trailer was kept full. We also filled the 20-pound propane tank, used for cooking, once a month. But the heat was no challenge and easily overcome by the bitter winds and sub-zero temperatures. Fearing for our existence during a particular cold spell, I took the children to my mother's farm and stayed for 10 days. The children wanted to go to the barn and play, but they could not reach the clothesline tethered to the back door of the kitchen to the barn. That tether was our lifeline so we would not be lost in the snow on the way to the barn to check on the animals and do chores. The farmhouse was a welcome respite from the tiny cold trailer. My mother generally had delivered, and went through three tons of coal, ordered from the coal mines. These would be delivered by truck that a miner would dump down a coal chute, located on the side of the house. This chute would reach a storeroom in the basement that also had a door. The door could be opened in the basement to shovel coal directly into the furnace. The furnace would be kept full of coal in the winter and required stoking about every four hours. But when it was stoked it would belch its welcome heat up into the vents to reach us through the floor registers, that the children huddled around.

My mother introduced the boys to "camping" by placing two chairs opposite each other and putting a sheet over it. The heat would come up into the tent, and the boys were occupied for hours, as they imagined what it would be like to camp. Of course, they were young, but I still remember the chatter and giggles of those boys as they spent hours in that tent. I was also incredibly grateful my mom was close and welcomed us to share her winter spoils. Cold spells would last about 4-6 weeks, with the worst of it being about week 4 and lasting roughly 10 days. After the 10th day I headed back to Minot to our little home on wheels. We had taken the advice from well-meaning strangers that turned out to be disastrous. They advised that we could keep the trailer warmer if we put straw under it. What did we know? We had no experience with this, but it sounded good at the time. We banked the bales of straw directly under the trailer and then sealed it with the skirting material, around the exterior, to keep the wind out. Like I said, I thought it was a good idea. Initially it did keep a lot of wind out and kept us warmer. But I had not anticipated who or what would move in during my 10-day absence.

When I got back to the Wigwam Trailer Park and put the boys to bed, I opened a cabinet and saw a tiny pair of eyes staring back at me. We both let out an eek! I slammed the door shut and opened the oven and saw several sets of legs scampering away. The entire trailer was inhabited by field mice that appreciated their new home far more than I did chasing them out of it. They found the straw under the trailer accessible and cozy, but not as warm and cozy as the inside of the cabinets, or in the oven! I battled this for a few days until Dutch came back and we put traps everywhere, but we were afraid the boys might get in one and accidentally set it off on themselves - or each other. After being advised we would have to remove the bales under the trailer and then fumigate, we had no choice but to go to the farm and stay with my mom again until we could go back in.

Fred and Sam thought this was a great adventure and got their overnight bag together to ready themselves to go into the cold out to the car. Rod was a toddler, so he required being picked up. This suited him just fine since he was happiest being held. This may explain why he was a late bloomer to walking. When we got back, I was grateful that the trailer had been cleaned up, although I cautiously opened the cabinet doors for quite a while. Once the skirting was removed the field mouse hotel was closed for business, as they preferred warmer digs.

As the winter left and the signs of spring arrived, work was plentiful, and we readied our plans for a new trailer to accommodate our growing family. We had about six or seven weeks before our next baby was due. In the first week of April our brand new, not used, mobile home was delivered to a brand-new mobile home park. Our little 28-foot trailer was used as down payment, mice and all, since we could not get them all out and they were reproducing. Oh Lord!

The new park, Pierce's Mobile Home Park, had nice big lots, with a slab foundation and utility hookups. The park had sidewalks, a community-center where you could pick up your mail and meet neighbors or do laundry. Our space was close to the community house, which was convenient for me, with the wash house on the other side of the building, always accessible and heated.

Early May 8th I woke my husband up and said it was time to go to the hospital. The boys were left with a babysitter we were fortunate to find directly across from us. I say fortunate because it was just after midnight. In that day, we did not have the modern conveniences available today like, ultrasound or amniocentesis. We would not know the sex or health of our baby until its birth. As we headed to the hospital, I remembered praying, "God please give me a girl. I want a little girl so bad. I have three boys and it would be such a miracle to have a girl. With hair that I can comb and dress like a little doll." At almost 9 lbs., Dr. Hurley exclaimed, "My! This is one big baby!"

This was an easier delivery than my previous three. Even though Fred was only 4.10 lbs., he was my first born and I had no prior experience to compare this to. And with him, it was a very long labor, starting at 7 am until his delivery at 7 pm. Fred was also 6 weeks early and the circumstances were so different then. Sam and Rod were heavier at approximately 7.3 lbs. and 6.8 lbs., respectively.

When that baby was handed to me, she looked half again the size of my other three. I was flooded with joy as Dr Hurley delighted in telling me I had a 9 lb. baby girl! Her head was so full of hair – not like any of the boys – and instantly looked like the most beautiful baby I had ever seen. As I was taken out of the delivery room my heart swelled with the pride only a new mom can have – but this was a special girl-filled swelling. As soon as my husband arrived at 7 am I asked him to rush out and call my mother to announce, it's a girl!

It was a bright and warm day and there was a special feeling of joy in the air. I could hardly wait the five days I would be kept in the hospital to get home and share my new bundle of joy with the rest of my family. Of course, my mother wasted no time, as she excitedly put the announcement, "She got her wish!" into the local paper, The Daily News.

When I brought Linda home, I was greeted at the door with the squealing delight of the boys. Everyone was fascinated with her. Fred would hold her, careful not to touch the top of her head, playing with the curls of hair falling below her ear. He enjoyed tickling her feet and telling me how much bigger his feet were than hers. Sam would stare at her and sneak looks and smile when he was caught looking. Rod was more stand-offish now with some competition for my lap and hip. Dutch enjoyed holding her because, unlike Rod who cried a lot, she was quiet and seemed to sense that she was the show, even then. He would sit in the rocking chair and just rock her until she fell asleep, which was fast.

Frequently I would pick her up out of his arms while Dutch slept too and put her to bed. Rod and Linda slept in the stroller, a small investment when we got it for Fred, but it was getting plenty of use. It was deep and could be unhooked and made into a bed. We could also detach the bed and put it into the car. When Linda was about 18 months she crawled out of the stroller and told her lingering brother Rod, still in the stroller, "Come on Rodney, let's go in the house." She had already started to show early signs of being Fred's replacement, as he handed the broom to her and said, "Here, Linda, you can sweep the floor now!" Fred had been a really good helper, but he knew talent when he saw it and welcomed the relief of Linda's help, which Sam and Rod showed no interest in whatsoever.

The trailer was twice as big as the previous one, it had two bedrooms, lots of closet space, a separate living room, and finally, an indoor toilet, unlike the 28-foot trailer before. The kids' bedroom had two sets of bunkbeds. But despite the size of our new dwelling, it was still small enough for me to keep a watchful eye on the kids as they raced up and down the trailer or played hide and seek.

Having a girl changed the dynamics in the family. I had no idea what a blessing she would be then, and throughout my life. I would have accepted another boy but having three boys already I longed for a girl. We were content. We had enough food and enough work to get a new home, but I had not anticipated the joy would extend beyond our little nucleus. My older sister, Edna, who had moved to New Mexico years earlier, had a daughter the same age as Fred but had a strained relationship with her mother and did not visit. Linda was the first granddaughter my mother could hold. My mother made beautiful dresses for Linda so I could dress up my little doll. That beautiful dressmaking by my mother would continue through Linda's teens. My younger sister, Donna, would also delight in this new little girl. Mom and Donna had both been excited for me as I had each of my boys, but I believe they shared the same excitement I had now. Boys seem to be a little tougher – especially having them close in age. But girls – you handle differently, gentler. Oh, thank heaven for little girls.

Within six months my husband had an opportunity to work in Rochester, MN on the construction of a new hospital. That meant he would be spending the cold winter working inside a building and getting a steady paycheck. This required moving his family close by. The trailer was moved by a professional moving company, and the rest of us scurried to the Hudson, with a dashboard that required a few phone books to see over the steering wheel. Rochester is about 585 miles southeast of Minot and would require a full day's drive to get there, with no stops. That would not have been possible with four kids though. I remember sitting in the back so I could change the two youngest so we would have fewer stops. We did not have money to stay in a hotel and stopping at a diner was out of the question. This would have required the logistical skills of a Field Marshall and I was not up to the task.

As the sun set the kids easily fell asleep and I was able to sit with my husband and keep him awake as we happily talked about our dreams, plans for the winter, and the new baby on the way. Before we left Minot, I had been upset with my doctor's religious response to my request for birth control. We had discussed the failed attempts that resulted in two previous pregnancies and I was too young for a more permanent solution. Suggesting that I simply abstain was hardly sound medical advice. I was concerned about the many mouths we had to feed and the growing responsibility of raising this size of a family. I was alarmed but Dutch reminded me that every child is a gift from God and each and every one of them a miracle of life. As I rested on his shoulder, I appreciated he saw this as our blessing and that we were in this together. Our needs were met, we had a new roof over our heads, and the kids were small enough to easily manage keeping the family together. I think Dutch secretly liked the idea of traveling to a new destination, as long as the family was together.

The company my husband worked for provided a campsite, with hookups for the electricity and plumbing. This was a totally new adventure for the growing boys. Fred and Sam would take their toy dump trucks out and mimic the ones they saw. Many times, we went to the zoo where the kids really enjoyed seeing all the animals. They would imitate their favorite animal sounds to their dad when he came home. I am not sure if it was the zoo visits that planted a seed of having our own animal or not, considering there would be one more thing to clean up after, but we got our first dog, Cookie, named by the boys. Cookie was aptly named as a treat the kids wanted, because you have never seen so much love given to an animal as Cookie got. First Fred would pet, then Sam would play, then Rod would pet and give a treat, then Linda would comb, then repeat. Cookie was in heaven on earth.

I am not sure if it was the sudden Minnesota weather change or the calling to the kids or combination of the two that caused it, but I lost my voice. Suddenly I could not speak louder than a whisper and could not raise my voice, much to the delight of the kids and my husband! I went to the Mayo Clinic, alarmed that I may have to consider being like this for the rest of my life. They ran a full week of tests, for both my skin and my throat. Of course, they were also concerned about my pregnancy, and wanted to find a solution as soon as possible. They discovered nodes on my vocal cords that would heal without surgery if I followed the prescribed protocol. My voice stayed at a whisper for the next three months. I worried about the Mayo Clinic's billing. Although my husband had steady work, a big medical bill would set us back financially. When I went to pay the bill so many things were going through my mind that I barely heard the receptionist say, "That'll be $10.00 ma'am." I was startled and said, "$10.00 a month?" "No. That's the total bill." God surely had His hand on me as I counted out my change - and my blessings over and over again out of the building, into the car, all the way home, over and over again, thanking God.

We were in Rochester about six months before the next big job assignment. It is easy to move a small family so young. They think everything is an adventure. For me, because we were in a mobile home, it was far easier than it would have been, say, for a military family who would have to pack up all their belongings and move to another city or state or even country. We called the same moving company that had moved us from Minot to Rochester and we were fortunate to move to a park that was owned by the same owners of the park in Minot. The park was new and beautiful with all the then-modern facilities.

Prenatal care was similar to what it is today, to a point. Come in, weigh in, listen to the heartbeat, get lectured if you gained more than 20 lbs., and take your prenatal pills. After Linda was born, I did not see a doctor until I was six months pregnant with my next child. We were fortunate that the two previous children, and now a third, were born after the tax refunds were issued. We had the money to pay for these deliveries in cash. In late July, my husband took me over the Red River bridge from Moorhead to Fargo, about five miles, to deliver our next son, James.

Men were not allowed to be a part of the birthing process, missing out on the bonding that comes with the new arrival of your bundle of joy. Instead, Dutch hurried back to relieve the babysitter and stay with the four children for the next 5 days. Again, North Dakota required 5 days of rest, with extraordinarily little walking we know today is necessary. Then, we were encouraged to rest somewhat before the real chores began. I was bound with a canvas material as tight as a corset, to encourage the muscles to remember to restore my youthful figure more quickly. This had been done after each of the previous 4 pregnancies and was something I did not look forward to. We were then instructed to do a few exercises, all while bound, so that I looked as forward to getting out of there as my family looked forward to having me come home. It was remarkable how quickly James adapted to his new environment. He immediately slept 6 hours – without the required nighttime feeding assignments my husband and I had shared with the previous 4 kids. We were all grateful for this.

With work getting ready to furlough for the winter we headed back to Minot, to the same park we had occupied the previous year. There we remained for the next two years.

As James got older, he started to run with his older brothers up and down the trailer, requiring less and less sleep as he got older. He bored easily and constantly wanted some sort of stimulation which, for a while, was running up and down the trailer. One early fall morning I was in the kitchen when James called out to me that he was going to get up. He slept on the top of one of the sets of bunk beds. Before I could get down the length of the trailer, he jumped off the top bunk. I picked him under his arms and his legs dangled as if they were not connected to his tiny torso. Thank goodness my husband was home, and he ran across the way to get a babysitter. I could not put James down, I was too afraid to move him, as I cradled him into my arms. I knew it was something broken because I remembered breaking my own wrist years earlier and had observed my own wrist's similar detachment. I honestly cannot recall anything except that I needed to get to the hospital with him ASAP. We rushed into the emergency room of the closest hospital and they immediately knew what happened.

The doctors took him to get x-rayed. I sat expectantly waiting for the doctor to come back and report what had to be done. When the doctors came, they told us that James had broken his pelvis and would require a body cast for the next several weeks.

Although they encouraged me wait in the waiting room, I was not about to leave the spot I had left James in until the doctors returned him to me. When James's cast had been newly outfitted, we collected him. He was about 2-1/2 years old and he was so tiny in that large plaster-of-Paris cast.

The body cast conveniently had a changing station built into it. We had just gotten him out of diapers and suddenly, we were back to basics. The cast went all the way down his legs and were separated to hold his legs in place by a bar. There was a small curvature at the back so we could partially recline him. He was a total oddity to the kids.

We were all so stunned that this had happened that we all remained very still and quiet for days. When something like this happens, you think about what you were doing and how you could have prevented it. A lot of "shoulda, coulda, wouldas" went over and over through my mind. I was mortified to take my broken baby boy to the doctors. Although James was the youngest, he wanted to be up on the top bunk so he could climb up the sides like a monkey - until then.

In retrospect James was a willful child – "I'm going to get down!" he exclaimed, despite my urging him to stay put until I came in. What happened in seconds seemed like hours as I replayed this scene over and over again in my mind. The doctors questioned both my husband and me, making sure there was an abusive environment did not exist. Of course, there was not, but I was immediately harder on myself than the situation called for. I took the blame then and avowed something like this would never happen again on my watch.

We previously had insurance with a large insurance carrier but because there was a long waiting period – frequently 90 days from the start of the job – that before we had paid for the premiums and qualified for the insurance - we would have a new job site to go to, preventing us from being able to qualify for insurance. In order to qualify my husband had to work so many days in a row. This was tough, given the circumstances of short- term assignments. In any event we knew we would not be able to afford the bill without me going back to work to help pay this. Getting an administrative job at the hospital, I stayed with the kids during the day and, when my husband came home at 4:30pm, I would leave for work. My shift, from 5 pm till 1am was hard on mostly my husband. He hated that I had to work and stayed awake until I got home.

We continued to talk about California, mostly as a diversion from the nighttime work assignment. He worried for me about coming home so late. We did not have cell phones or even a landline in the home, so he worried about things I would have never thought about like a tire going flat, or being safe getting to the car, or even falling asleep on the way home.

As soon as I made the last payment on the hospital bill, I came home elated. As excited as I was to share this news, my husband had his own excited announcement. "How soon can you be ready? We are leaving North Dakota."

Lord, I'll Never Forget Lodi

What then shall we say
of these things? If God
be for us, who can be
against us?

ROMANS 8:31 (KJ21)

70

Chapter 7

Lord, I'll Never Forget Lodi

It was September 26, 1957

After four bitterly cold winters in North Dakota, we knew we could not spend another winter there. On Wednesday nights I attended my church's homegroup, a study and prayer group, that today might be considered a life group.

This group met at Pastor Heilig's home, and we prayed for things we heard the need for or knew of. I took my burden of needing direction on where we would head to this group. We fervently prayed for God's direction, that we would be led to the right place – for our safe journey.

We just knew that we could not remain in North Dakota. There was just too much winter and not enough work. Many a night my husband and I knelt and held hands and earnestly prayed for merciful direction. We regularly tithed, something we faithfully continued throughout our marriage, and waited on God's mercy. We thought about Montana, but winter was harsh there too. We had discussed California because I had family in San Diego. Plus, it was warm year-round – and there would be work. My husband remembered Central California, when he was in the service and wanted no part of it. After some discussions and a lot of prayer we headed for California. Those nights of uncertainty made our resolve with God even stronger.

We had $500 to our name when we left North Dakota. We were optimistic this would cover all our costs. It wasn't much of a stretch since gas was $.25 a gallon; a loaf of bread was $.15. We stopped every few hours for the kids to get out and run around. When we were tired of traveling for the day, we pulled into campgrounds dotted throughout our travel. These were sparse with room to park the rig, use a public bathroom, rest, and leave. These were not well-maintained campgrounds, but they were free and gave us a place for the kids to play, hopefully using up all their unbound energy before we started the next leg of the journey.

Sleeping in the trailer was not an adventure for the kids because that's where they lived. But the fact that their home was mobile bringing us to a new location every night was new. And because they dreamed of our destination, California and picking oranges off trees we often told them about, they could not wait to get there too.

We talked about the oranges and the sunshine in California we were going to. Sitting at the table after a meal was prepared was all about the stories and what we would be doing in California.

We had not anticipated the cost of relocation. Although we had planned for our travel expenses we had not planned for the cost of the many mechanical breakdowns. We had not gotten far, but into the next state, when the pickup truck's radiator had to be replaced. Minot, North Dakota to Rapid City, South Dakota is about 394 miles. Traveling about 45 mph we had travelled a full day at least. It cost $55, which does not sound like much today. But at this point we had used 20% of our travel funds on food, gas and now the unexpected cost of repair. We were very aware of the need to watch our costs as we continued to travel.

We travelled in a 1950 one-ton truck as we pulled a 45-foot-long trailer behind it. Ha! A modern-day version of a covered wagon with all the 1957 conveniences including clean clothes daily, an indoor toilet, beds to sleep in and a stove to cook on.

We were all stuffed into the cab of that truck. It would be decades before safety rules for car seats, headrests or even seatbelts would exist.

I marvel at this fact today. Federal seat belt law did not go into effect before 1968! Good thing the kids were small. One was on my lap, and we had our own four-on-the-floor version of day care.

We were on a two-lane highway in the middle of Wyoming where it was rare to see another car for over an hour of driving. It was an easy drive to get the truck up to 45-50 mph without having to slow down. The wind was blowing hard, pelting the windshield with what little tumbleweed vegetation there was, along with a flurry of dirt clouds and gravel. Getting behind a slow truck or rig meant we had a slowdown, wait for a clearing in the oncoming traffic before we could safely pull into the oncoming lane, then speed up to overcome and pass the slower rig. If we were not fast enough, we would end up in the same place behind the same rig to avoid a head-on collision.

It was four o'clock in the afternoon and the sun was setting fast. We had been trying to make good time to get to the next stop, a small Wyoming town's mobile park campsite for the night. We were still miles from our night's destination when Dutch felt the trailer pull hard, suddenly, in the opposite direction of the steering wheel. Instinctively he knew that one of the trailer's tires had blown out. He yelled, "Hold the kids tight! We're starting to swerve!" We were going maybe 45 mph and you might as well have said 100. If the trailer that was whipping in the opposite direction of our truck was not brought under control we would get pulled under, along with the trailer, if it flipped over.

We frequently prayed out loud and this was no time for an exception. I prayed, "God! Help us. Hear my plea!" I repeated this and I began to hear Dutch say it too. Cars were honking at us as they passed in the opposite direction, as if we did not know we were in danger.

Time seemed to suspend as if a second was minutes and everything else was in slow motion. Fred and Sam put their small arms around my neck and hung on for dear life. Rod was on the floor and unaware of the certain death we were all facing. Linda was in my arms and James was next to me and woke up to the calamity of Fred and Sam crying, his father yelling danger sounds he had never heard and us praying a plea to God to save us, and he started crying too. Dutch's superpower was nerves of steel and the strength of calm as we were all headed to a certain predictable fate. He miraculously slowed the truck down without letting it get whipped out of control by the trailer which caused the steering wheel to literally vibrate violently.

The thought of the dishes that must have flown out of the cabinets and the broken things in the trailer left on the table were the farthest thing from my mind, as I continued to hold my children tightly and plead for God's mercy. The kid's heads were buried somewhere on my body, and I was still praying for the hand of God to save us when a hand touched my arm. Thinking I had surely perished and had arrived at the Gate of Heaven with my children, I opened my eyes. In that moment I saw my husband and the anguished relief on his face that he had finally stopped this roller coaster of a double-axle trailer from killing all of us. A double axel means there are just two tires on each side of this behemoth 45-foot long, 10-foot-wide beast of a trailer. We laughed. We cried. We thanked God for this merciful sparing of our lives. There is nothing like a little hardship to get us to submit to a routine of prayer. And you do not have to wait for a trailer whipping out of control to do it daily. But it is in those moments when you have been brought through a near disaster you are grateful for that routine. Try it out and find how easy it is. You do not need to wait for a disaster!

Wyoming is a fairly flat state, and the highway provided a pull-out area on the side of the road. This miraculous and divine intervention had provided a safe place for us to disconnect the entire trailer from the truck. After some time, the truck was free to backtrack to the previous, but larger, town to replace the irreparable tire.

Dutch left but it was my job to put order back in place, so I fed the kids and put them to bed. Without a thought about the trailer's proximity to the road's passing traffic, without lane markers, emergency blinkers, reflectors or even flares I lit a single candle, placing it on the sink sideboard, and quietly waited for Dutch to return. The simple red cotton bandana flag attached to the side of the trailer would hopefully prevent an alert driver from running into the back of us.

In the stillness, I reflected on the events of the day. I was secure in my faith and my husband depended on my belief and the strength of my own faith for his. He would ask, "Do you think we're going to make it through this" and my answer always was, "Yes!" The same blind faith that journeyed with my ancestors was surely in my DNA. I truly believed that God would bring us safely to where we were going.

It was that same blind faith that allowed me to trust in the process – so much that I did not give it a second thought that I was alone in Wyoming with five children in a trailer on the side of the road without a dime in my possession. But back then, my husband oversaw the money and carried it all with him. I had plenty to think about with five young children, so I was relieved money allocation was not my responsibility.

It never occurred to me about what I would do if he never made it back. I trusted he would be and that all would be well. Credit cards, gas cards, gift cards or checks did not exist. In God we trust. All others pay cash.

This is a good time to remind you that it is fine to have someone take care of you and look out for you, but this is a new century! And you need to know something about finances if you do not already have this knowledge. Know where things are and how they work. You'll gain confidence in this knowledge and not leave you at someone else's mercy. Thankfully I did not have to utilize this knowledge.

Three hours had passed, and it was dark. With the kids asleep, I wondered if he was lost. How hard could it be to find a tire? My young mind did not know the answers. I just waited in the dark trailer, with the one small candle on the sink counter to over-shadow the thoughts that were going through my head. It did not occur to me that he would have to go to several places to find the right sized-tire or the equipment to change it, so late in the afternoon. Steel belted tires did not exist. It was a tubed tire.

Sometimes a blessing is disguised as a problem. When he finally came back, he was followed by a worker in a second truck. As it turned out, a special jack was required to lift the trailer to change the tire. We were told these tires were never meant to provide more than mobilization into place in a park – and not for cross country travel.

We would not have found the kind of help we needed in the small town we had been headed towards. We were very fortunate to find the help needed but it had a cost. $70 was totally unexpected and we were now halfway down on our travel funds. My husband was very worried. We had spent six hours fixing a problem and more money than we had planned. He must have thought, "Here we are, on the side of the road in Wyoming, with five kids and one on the way, a wife, a new trailer and not so new truck. Why is this happening? Will we make it there? What was I thinking?" He was the strong and silent type but after the $70 was counted out, the worker left with a bologna sandwich I had made for him and the memory of my husband repeatedly uttering the same sentiment, "$70.00??" under his breath with a far-off gaze.

It was after midnight when my husband finally crawled into bed. But it was a fitful sleep, and we were on the road again before dawn. He had it in his mind that we needed to get over Donner's Pass before it snowed. And at this time of year, it was a real concern. After two mechanical breakdowns it is a wonder that we did not have our own emotional breakdowns. We continued our journey in silence.

In those days, if you had a radio, signal strength was not strong enough to get much more than static. Without an iPhone podcasts or streaming services so popular today we usually had our own talk and chatter or occasional song to break the silence. But on that occasion, I prayed the thoughts in our heads would not become words. It was a long way to Nevada, and I remember looking at the side of the road a lot, afraid to look over at my husband's determined face.

It was day four on the road when we stopped to feed the kids and rest. It was raining, cold and grey. As I opened the door of the trailer the smell of dirty laundry was overpowering. Disposable diapers did not exist, but a few days on the road meant we needed to find a washer. I was grateful that only one child was still in diapers. Laundromats did not exist and finding a commercial laundry facility was challenging.

We drove until we found a trailer camp. It was $2/night, but it had 2 Maytag wringer washers (a danger that I still shudder at the thought of today), commercial dryers, toilets that flush and a place for the kids to play. Maybe it was the respite from the road trip or being cooped up in a truck with 5 kids under the age of 7, but my husband volunteered to take on the laundry task. He was always a good helper. The rest of us could eat, get cleaned up and have a good long nap. Right! Those kids had so much energy I now wish I could have figured out how to bottle it in an updated version of Lydia Pinkham's tonic! Mac and cheese were not in a box with hydrated cheese. It was made from scratch, with a side of bologna sandwich. And this took a little more time to prepare. We were Somewhere, USA - between Wyoming and Nevada.

Day five put us on course for going through Donner's Pass. Again, it was late in the afternoon when we met with a new challenge. We were stopped by State Troopers on what is today's Interstate 80. They asked us if we had chains.

They had to ask a few times because as soon as one of the kids started to cry, they were all crying. We were able to confirm we had one set of chains for the truck but not for the trailer. They told us we would not be able to go over the Pass because it had already started snowing.

After hours of being cooped up, the kids wanted to get out, but when they heard the State Trooper say we could not go on they all began to wail in a chorus of lament. They begged the Troopers to let us go through to California. The oldest child, Fred, explained how tired he was of being in the truck with all his siblings and if we could only get to California maybe the snow would stop.

Maybe it's the magic-thinking and simplicity of a child's mind but they honestly believed California was the promised land, and knew it was just on the other side of the hill. It may have been the begging, pleading, and wailing of the children or maybe the exhausted expression on my husband's and my face, but in a moment the Troopers relented. They agreed to let us go through, but we had to buy a second set of chains. Pulling over to have them installed by another big rig truck cost us more of the very little funds we had left.

Be careful what you ask for because you just might get it. Donner's Pass is a mountain pass in northern Sierra Nevada, above Donner Lake, and about 9 miles west of our next destination, Truckee, California. Like the Sierra Mountain range themselves, this is a very steep pass.

You can read more about this on the website, www.dangerousroads.org to get a better idea of what we were experiencing, only then it was still a two-lane highway, 7,056 feet above sea level.

After the chains were put on, in retrospect, we began the most dangerous part of the journey. We had already seen the unexpected depletion of our funds and the reality of mechanical breakdowns. As my husband tensely grabbed the steering wheel and I held the children tightly, we inched our way along, with the state trooper close behind us, until we got to the pass.

We were on our own after that. Call it the folly of our youth or faith and belief that nothing bad would happen, we pressed on. Despite that, I never saw the forest through the trees of the Tahoe National Forest. Possibly because of the snow or my eyes shut so tightly while I prayed. When we got to the top of the hill, we were somewhat relieved until we started our descent down the hill. It was fervently on my mind that if another tire blew or our brakes gave out, we would all perish. The words of the hymn, "God will take care of you" went over and over in my mind as I repeated the words…

Without the Avalanche warnings you can read about online or the steel-belted tires or options to pull over that exist today, we did not heed the advice of the State Trooper to wait it out a few days.

After hours, which seemed like days, we finally got over and down the pass safely. I have not been on that road ever since. It only takes one time to be that thankful, grateful, and tired and to remind yourself that your faith in God is the one that is tested and not the other way around. When I think of the danger we faced and our own naivety I now realize I may have been testing God's mercy.

Hindsight is always 20/20. Even a child challenges whether the flame will burn or not, and despite the warning of the State Trooper, my childlike mind never believed we would not make it through.

After a very arduous journey cross country we arrived in CA on October 2. Being advised of the cities we could stop and look for day work in California we continued south. After another day and a half, we arrived in Lodi late Saturday afternoon. We pulled into the Twin Palms trailer park with its own fruit and vegetable stand. The kids' eyes were as big as the cantaloupes they ate as we enjoyed our first night in Southern California.

After the kids were put to bed, my husband shared that we were down to our last $5…enough to fill the task of the truck but not the bottomless pit of the kids' stomachs the next day. I was four months pregnant with our sixth child and I now feared for our future in a place that might as well have been as far away as my ancestor's homeland in Russia. I walked, wept, and prayed.

As I thanked God for our safe journey, I petitioned Him for a job to emerge for my husband. With my head down, so passers-by did not see me weeping, I continued to pray. As I finished my amen, I slowly opened my eyes with resolve and saw a piece of paper on the ground. It was a $20-dollar bill! I turned it over and over and over again in my hand in total disbelief! Thanking God for His abundance and mercy I knew God's hand was on me.

The grocery store was not far from the park, and I immediately went there and bought provisions. Hauling 5 lbs. of sugar, 5 lbs. of flour, meat, butter, bread and yeast in paper bags I still had about $16 left. Enough to put gas in the tank and maybe something left over for the kids!

My husband had been waiting for me to return, knowing how upset I was when I left. The worry on his face turned to wonder then amazement as he saw me carrying those bags. When I told him exactly how this happened, he shared this miracle and joy with me. My thoughts turned to wanting to be in a house of praise and worship and to place the $2.00 tithe into the collection plates. On Sunday morning we packed everyone into the truck. Without the internet to do a Google search we merely sought the closest church to not waste gas. It turned out to be a Baptist church.

My husband volunteered to take the kids back to the trailer park while he did some chores and left me there. With my Bible tucked under my arm I sought a pew near the back of the small church. It was peaceful and I quietly enjoyed the sense of the miraculous in that moment. At the close of the service, a woman that sat next to me greeted me and asked if I was from North Dakota. You can imagine how surprised I was at this question, and I wondered why I kept seeing her glance at me and at once at my bible. She appeared to me to be about thirty-five or forty. Although I did not instantly recognize her, she asked me about my father, Samuel and mother, Sophie.

At this point I asked her how she knew this information about me. It had not occurred to me that she had been looking at my maiden's name, Lorraine Harchanko, engraved on the outside of my Bible. Her German father, who spoke fluent Russian, had been the minister of the local church in Max, a really small town. He had even been my mandolin instructor! She had grown and left that same small town we had just come from but what are the odds of meeting someone from your hometown? Was it a mere coincidence or was this another example of Divine intervention? She hurriedly asked me why I was in Lodi. After some explanation I said that we had heard harvests were year-round and we had come in search of work in the fields.

She explained that only grapes were in season, then oranges, but they would not be ready for a few months. When I asked if she knew anyone that needed help, she told me her sister and husband owned vineyards. After calling her sister, Doris and her husband came to the trailer park and invited my family to their home for a very welcoming Sunday dinner. My husband's job started that Monday.

I marvel at the many wonders and miracles I have had in my life, but Lodi stands out as one of my most memorable periods. It was our real first stop.

We were broke and needed a place to stay. The Trailer Park extended credit and we were instantly received. We needed food and were surrounded by fields of vegetables and fruit stands. We needed money and I miraculously "found" $20. I needed to be spiritually fed and found a home with family in a faraway place. We needed a job and found it.

Within a week we had enough money to leave this park and head to our final destination, San Diego.

It was warm in Lodi and no snowshoes were needed. To us it was like summer.

Should I See A Doctor?

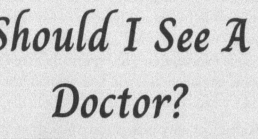

Doc, I think I have internal bleeding

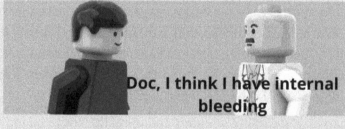

That's where the blood's supposed to be

Surely there is a balm in the land of Gilead. Surely there is a doctor there. So why aren't the hurts of my people healed?

Jeremiah 8:22 (ICB)

Chapter 8

Should I See a Doctor?

This was going to be our first winter in California and it was already the Promised Land I had hoped for. Going out in the late fall morning was like being in North Dakota on a summer morning. I could hardly believe it was already mid-October! Dutch and I could not get over the fact that everything was green – lawns, trees, the parks. You could just walk out the door in the fall or winter and get in your car and go wherever you wanted to drive. Driving out of the snow for the last time, over Donner's Pass, and seeing leaves on the trees and feeling how warm it was could only be described by this North Dakota girl as the most incredible feeling. Over the next several months we would be just like little kids and say to each other, "Look at this! Can you believe how green it is?" or "Can you believe that?!"

You did not have to get up in the morning and put on the snow gear to go out and scrape the snow off the sidewalks or deice the windshield or remove the head bolts, scarves, and mittens. Keeping the shovel in the back of the car in case you had to dig yourself out of the mud was going to be a way of life I could say good riddance to.

Severe minus 40 winters, summer bugs, mosquitos, immediate and sudden torrential storms, more mosquitos, then getting stuck in the mud again was something I would never miss.

With growing babies that needed to get outside and limited options to get to a zoo - if you could find one - meant we always had to deal with the harshness of the 6-month winter and 2-month summers. While initially this was part of our reason for leaving North Dakota, we also knew the costs associated with this harsh weather would be significantly reduced, if not eliminated altogether. No more gear, no more winter fuel bills, California here we are!

Although we had fewer bills, we still had to face the fact that we needed to find steady work. Dutch just needed good weather to work in and we believed we would find work immediately. The harvest work picking grapes was just enough money to make the payment on the trailer and the one-ton truck so we could keep on moving. The truck had been purchased just before we left North Dakota, specifically to pull the trailer. We traded the fully paid Hudson for the down payment. As we headed out of the Twin Palms Park in Lodi, we headed south.

After traveling for a few hours, we pulled into San Bernardino. It was just after 5 PM, and the sun was going down fast. We looked for a place to stay but were turned down at the first stop. We were advised to keep going on to Redlands, about 7 or 8 miles away. Purely by Divine providence we pulled into a park and were immediately welcomed.

Right next to the park was the equivalent of a YMCA. It was a big building that had loads of age-appropriate activities for the kids. Fred and Sam could go over at 1:00 in the afternoon and the kids, working on long picnic tables, would come back a few hours later with stories and completed arts and craft projects. Sam was already showing signs of artistry – carefully staying within the coloring lines.

In early November we were still at the same park and did not have the money to make the trailer or truck payments. Since we still needed funds to get to San Diego, Dutch worked the fall harvest, picking oranges and grapefruit.

Realizing making $7/day was not very fruitful, he wanted to get to the work he knew paid a fair wage. While Dutch headed to San Diego, hosted by my dad's sister and brother-in-law, Uncle Al and Aunt Kate, I stayed with the kids in Redlands. Uncle Al had a few connections and used them to request work on Dutch's behalf. Within a few days he went to work with a plaster company in Lemon Grove, a quiet suburb in San Diego.

Making enough money to pay just the truck's late charges and a partial trailer payment through November we continued to struggle. With money constraints getting harder I did my best to pitch in at the park and cleaned the public areas, in exchange for the rental space, to meet our obligations. We prayed harder than we ever did for God's hand to bless Dutch's work. And we did everything we could to prevent the risk of losing the roof over our head.

God is merciful and heard our prayers because the mortgage company accepted the interest only payment through the next February. That was such a blessing I still thank God for this miracle to this day.

After his first full week of work, Dutch came back to Redlands to bring provisions. At the end of that weekend, he headed back to San Diego in the truck.

By the second week he came back without the truck, driving a different car. When I asked him where the truck was, he shrugged and said, "GMC needed the truck more than we did." After two missed payments they came and took the truck. What he said next is the constant reminder of our daily walks with God and God's constant hand on us.

He said he walked over to a car lot on Broadway in Chula Vista. He told the salesman what had happened to his truck; that he had a family in Redlands, a wife that was 8 months pregnant, that he was employed - but he needed a car. With nothing but that story he drove an old Buick off the lot with $10 down, $10 a week for 9 weeks. That $100 car, with all the pings, dings and rattles was a constant reminder to say our prayers, as we fervently prayed that the car would make it over the grade from the then narrow highway 8 in San Diego to Redlands and back.

It was Christmas and it was going to be a meager one. There was no extra money for the usual feast of the holidays. In fact, we did not know if we would even have a holiday meal. I busied the kids with the left-over construction papers as they made the kitchen table Santa's workshop for the presents they were making for each other.

It was December 23, and I had just come back from my chores only to find a large paper bag on my doorstep. It was a tall but very full bag. To my amazement and the kids' excitement, it was full of toys and food. Cheese, flour, sugar, a can of pumpkin, toys, butter… but who gave this to us? Where did this come from? Who knew we needed this so badly? Tears of joy of the realization of yet another miracle and demonstration of God's abundance filled my eyes. Just like the Israelites, manna from the atmosphere literally appeared.

In January I came back to the trailer to find a Red Cross note on the door. A Red Cross nurse had left a message to call her back. Finding a public phone, I called the Red Cross. The nurse wanted to know if I had seen a doctor. I said I hadn't. She asked if I was taking prenatal pills. I said I had. With the previous children the prenatal care was the same except for the doctor visits. She asked if I had a place to have the baby. I said, "Yes, I guess I'll have the baby at home." My husband and I had talked about this, but we could not or would not think that far ahead. He may have been afraid to talk about it because he was worried about our financial situation and how he would pay for this birth. It had been a mere few months earlier that I had just paid off the hospital bill for James's broken hip and my husband wanted to make sure he could provide for his family without me going back to work. But I thought about my own mother having her children at home, with the help of a midwife. Having a baby at home did not seem so out of place, so I put it out of my mind. Growing up on a farm it was not uncommon for families to have 5 or 6 children. It was commonplace to have children at home, but I had had the luxury of having my children in a hospital. Although I did worry about giving birth and who would take care of cleaning up the baby, I was not concerned about me. Besides, this was an easy pregnancy so what could go wrong?

At first, I was confused about how the Red Cross knew, but then recalled talking about my pregnancy while working in the laundry room. "Someone must have called the Red Cross," I thought. The nurse's questioning continued. "Would you object to going to San Bernardino to see a doctor?" Of course, I would not object, but the reason why I had not seen a doctor yet was the harsh reality of our finances. Suddenly I was confronted with the fact that someone else thought I should see a doctor when I knew I could not afford to do that. Then, I would have to wait until my husband was home to drive me several miles to see the doctor, making this reality ever more profound. I was totally humiliated. While I fought back my own tears, I was protective of my unborn baby. "Should I see a doctor? What if something did go wrong?"

After she made the appointment, I thought about all of this while I waited until my husband was home at the weekend and could take me in. Before the children were up, or down for naps I prayed. Through my prayers, I tuned my heart to hear the whisper of God's voice. "Lean on me. Be not troubled. I will bring you through." In Psalms 27, I read, The Lord is the stronghold of my life. Of whom shall I be afraid? The Lord is my light and my salvation." And lean on Him, I did. Through those prayers I realized that my pride was injured, and the feelings of humiliation were coming from my pride. It was pride that kept me from even telling my family or my husband's family about this pregnancy. When I thought about how easy a family of any size would be to have with money, I narrowed my focus on my feelings of inadequacy on the lack of money. No one would dare ask a wealthy woman why she would have so many children, so why would this question someone asked me, when I picked up the boys, bother me so much? I was not expecting anyone to help us. When that red cross appeared at my door, I accepted the Red Cross's help, as the blessing it was.

After what seemed like hours at the clinic, I was called in. I was nervous and still embarrassed that I had not been to a doctor yet. But the doctor softly questioned me without judgement or harshness, and I felt myself relaxing that everything would work out. After examining me, he determined Sunday, April 6 would be the due date. He asked me to come back weekly. Unfortunately, I missed the remainder of the doctor visits because I did not have transportation, did not know anyone to ask for a ride and worried about what I would do with the other 5 kids. Dutch came home at the weekends so we were relieved that the schedule for the baby's delivery for a Sunday meant he could keep his plan to take the following week off to stay with the kids. We knew the time in the hospital was shorter than North Dakota's five-day requirement and thought I would only need to stay for three days – still an eternity when you have five kids at home and you know your place is right there with them.

Man plans and God laughs.

It was Tuesday, March 31 when my water broke. I had to go to a neighbor and ask her for a ride to the hospital. Fortunately, a grown daughter who lived with her came over to stay with the kids. My husband was already back in San Diego. When I arrived at the hospital the neighbor walked me in. What seemed like just a few minutes, my new baby boy arrived. To this day I do not recall my neighbor's name but do remember her warmth, southern accent, and her hospitality. She came and visited me after the delivery then headed back to help her daughter tend the rest of the kids. I went to the nurse's station that evening and asked if I could make a long-distance call to the father of the child. I called my aunt's house and spoke to Dutch. We had talked about names and nothing he suggested was suitable. He did say, "Whatever you do, do not name him after me." It was the end of the second day, and I was ready to check out. The nurse said the baby could not leave without being named, for public records. He was named Delmar, Jr., much to the protests of Delmar, Sr.

Miracles
On Our Doorstep

He performs wonders that cannot be fathomed, miracles that cannot be counted.

Job 5:9 (NIV)

Chapter 9

Miracles on Our Doorstep

It would be one more month in the town of Redlands, as we welcomed Delmar Jr. into his new family, before my husband announced he had found a place for us to move together as a family and was close to his work.

We readied the family for our final move to San Diego. No strangers to the benefits of hiring experts, we left the task of moving the trailer to a moving company.

As the trailer left, we headed on a scenic route to San Diego. At that time, I did not know any of the road names and getting on a highway meant you needed to know your numbers. We headed west onto the newly built I-10 freeway. Shortly after, we took the exit onto the I-15 freeway, southbound. Wanting to know more about our new state we stopped in a little town called Elsinore, to look at a map. Remember those? It was 1958 and GPS had yet to be discovered.

We saw a road sign for Lake Elsinore, as we were passing through the town and stopped to let the kids run and play around the Lake. I learned that it was the lowest point of the 42-mile San Jacinto River watershed – and this lake was where the San Jacinto River terminated.

We had been on a couple of drives to just look around on the weekends and the name San Jacinto brought a smile to my face. I was new to the correct pronunciation of California towns. I had to get used to pronouncing the J as an H, like "Hacinto," not "Jawcinto". Every once in a while, I would slip but quickly correct myself when I saw a frown if I incorrectly pronounced a word. If this was going to be my new home, I had to abandon sounding like a tourist real fast.

As we looked up towards the ridge, we could see the road that the map indicated would take us on the fastest route to the coast. I looked at that ridge and immediately thought about the last time we were on a ridge – it was Donner's Pass and it had been snowing about 6 months earlier. But we were not pulling the trailer and there was no snow in sight in this southern California town, so we proceeded over the very narrow and winding road. The sky was a beautiful blue as we began the climb up the ridge, and as far as I could see, there was no snow.

Highway 74, the Ortega Highway, had been built in 1934, and stretched 21 miles from where we were in Elsinore, to where we were going, in San Juan Capistrano. With all the twists and turns of the winding road, we stopped at several turnouts to marvel at the sudden elevation and the spectacular vistas. As we continued our drive the scenery went from desert landscape to lush green trees and we knew we were in another forest. A road sign would confirm we were entering the western side of the Cleveland National Forest.

The kids were not particularly interested in the scenery, but I pointed out the trees and the mountains and described what it would be like to see the ocean for the very first time. If you can imagine, me, who has never seen the ocean, is now describing this to her children. The one thing I wanted to help them visualize was the idea that a wave of water would race towards the beach -and that it could be fun to run up to and away from, but they had to be careful. They had no idea what a beach was, but they could imagine the biggest playground sand box they had ever seen, so that was the imagery we used.

As we got to the end of the Ortega Highway we could see a bridge over a valley area, that today is North South Interstate 5. We continued past the Mission at Capistrano. We were on our own mission to see the Pacific Ocean. We opened the windows and began to feel the coolness of what we now know is an ocean breeze. But the smell of the ocean began to lure us to the sea. We knew we were close and as we got excited so did the kids. I do believe my eyes were bigger than all of theirs put together when I caught my first glimpse of the ocean. Water, as far as you could see, was crystal blue and incredible white foam hit the shore as waves repeatedly brought water to the shore and pulled it back into the sea with a consistent rhythm of a song, just as I had described to the kids. I would breathe in that salt air and fill my lungs and just hold it in. It felt so good on my skin, after I could catch my breath. If you have never seen something and you see it for the first time – all you can say is awwhhhhh, wowwwwww!

As the Ortega Highway ended at the ocean another road would take us north or south. We turned onto the Coast highway, which was then called the 101. Today the 101 is a completely different route. But back then, this was the only route we would take for the next several years from San Diego to San Jose, when we would visit my husband's sister and her family.

We stopped at a place called Capistrano Beach, or Capo Beach. This was then called Dana Point. We saw a sign about tide pools and raced to see what a tide pool was. The kids squealed with delight as each one of them picked up a shell as they collected razor clams, corkscrew shaped shells, tiny ones, big ones. They could not hold all the shells their tiny hands collected. But they hauled them to the beach edge and stood there and stared at the waves as they methodically came in and went back out. Nothing could have prepared us for the total fascination the tide pool provided though. The crystal-clear salt water revealed its treasures in these pools. I was completely overwhelmed when I held a starfish that covered my entire hand. The kids thought I was kidding – how could that star be a fish? When I turned it over to reveal its under-belly, we were amazed at the hundreds of projections that moved as it bristled in the sunlight.

I could have stayed there all day, but the kids were hungry, and we needed to find food and get back on the road so we could meet the trailer's arrival in San Diego.

We headed out onto the Cabrillo Highway, today known as Pacific Coast Highway, to one of the burger stands dotted along our path. No big-name McDonalds or Burger King would be commercially viable for a few more years. The roadside burger stands, where you could get 5 kid's burgers, two adult size burgers, 3 fries and 3 milkshakes for under $2.00, would fill us until we got to San Diego.

We continued south on the 101 until we got onto something called the Pacific Highway. From there, the names continually changed as we headed south on our journey. As we got closer to San Diego, we found ourselves on Torrey Pines Road, leading to La Jolla Blvd, all a part of the then 101 freeway. As we drove south through these little towns, we saw business districts and an occasional traffic light. These towns, connected by the roads we were on, were interchangeably called 101 or Pacific Coast Highway. That was confusing and I am sure this led to the renaming and expansion of roads seen throughout San Diego today.

We knew we were close when we crossed a bridge on Crosby Street. As we crossed the bridge, we quickly rolled up the windows. We learned this was where the tuna fleet came in with their haul and the Star-Kist tuna plant's processing aroma was proof of their catch. Wow what a smell you tried not to inhale deeply on. Short breaths and pedal to the metal was our survival tactic. In the late 1950's tuna was San Diego's third largest industry behind the Navy and aerospace. It employed some 40,000 San Diegans, catching, canning, and marketing the canned "chicken of the sea". Two of the three big canning companies were based in San Diego, where Bumble Bee Tuna is still processed. There were four canneries and so many fishing boats along the harbor that Seaport Village now occupies. To us though, it was just nasty smelling.

The kids marveled at the ships being built as we passed the National Steel and Shipbuilding, at 28th and Harbor Drive, where it still exists on San Diego Bay. Between the tuna and the 'rendering plant' (the slaughterhouse) at 24th Street we all held our breath for what seemed like an hour as we tucked our heads into anything we could do to block those awful smells. This never changed for us until the rendering plant and most of the tuna processing plants were retired.

Another two miles and we finally reached our destination. We turned off the road and crossed the newly built Palm Avenue Bridge. We crossed that Bridge and weaved through Palm City. We passed all the fields of tomatoes and alfalfa being grown. The two-way dirt gravel road took us to our final turn onto Palomar and we could see our mobile home park right ahead of us.

When we pulled up to our mobile home, we were delighted to see that everything had been set up for us. The mobile home was on its slab foundation; and the electricity, water and sewer were all hooked up. All we had to do was park and go inside. Our little home also had a yard enclosed by a little white picket fence. The kids would be able to play on the green grass of our patio while I hung up the clothes on our own clothesline. But now I had a real sense of being home. We were finally in San Diego, where I had secretly wanted to go for years. We were so thankful that we had arrived – not one child had a sickness, or an injury – something I still marvel at today.

Our first order of business was to find our church. We found it within a mile at Castle Park Baptist Church. The congregants were warm and welcoming. They marveled that we had come so far and to find our new church home with them. I was grateful for the nursery that Del Jr. and James went to so I could sit with my husband during the service. There were classes for the rest of the kids and having that brief reprieve from child watching let my arms rest and I could focus on the service.

Bringing these many youngsters to a relatives' house was something that never entered my mind. But bringing them to a house of worship with so many welcoming arms to take the kids on a biblical adventure gave us the encouragement to get involved with the congregation.

Dutch was immediately drawn to those that needed help. He had befriended the Delaney couple in their mid to late 50's. They had had one son, who had been killed in WWII, and had been members of the church for many years. This man had gotten cancer that quickly advanced, forcing him to sell his gas station and business on Third Avenue. Dutch visited him twice a week and helped him to get back and forth from his bed after a chemo treatment that had left his body so weak. Ravaged from the progressing disease that eventually took the man's life, I was happy to see my husband helping a family that needed help. We always remember the kindness of strangers because it is so unexpected. We had received more than our fair share of help from strangers and had been so grateful. Especially in Redlands. And every time I had gotten any kind of help in my husband's absence, I made sure I told him about this. So, at the first opportunity he could, he would touch the life of another human in need. Repeating that cycle throughout our lives has continued to remind me to be a vessel for God.

Even then, Chula Vista was quickly changing. The trolley that ran the length of Third Avenue, from downtown San Diego to Chula Vista had been taken out in 1957, the year before we arrived. That is the same year my dad's mother, Mora Harchanko, my grandmother, passed away. She had moved to San Diego in the early 40's to live with her daughter Kate and husband, Al Menard, after her husband died. I remembered her well. She had locked up all the vittles at sundown every Friday, until sundown on Saturday. She would suspiciously poke through her food, as a guest in my childhood home, refusing to eat anything with pork in it. I do not ever recall seeing her smile but remember how very small she was.

She silently took the trolley two times a week. Venturing out she had memorized her change and her stops. Perhaps it was the thought of her silent independence going away, or the possibility of having to learn English at the age 98, her life was suddenly shortened. Mora Harchanko never learned to speak English and conversed almost exclusively with her daughter in Russian. The only thing Moriah translated fluently was the US currency. She kept her own bank in the "Upper B of A" or in a sock in the bottom drawer and kept her own garden until her death at 99. She had a unique way of warding off the spirits of poverty, and she knew where she had stashed every coin she placed throughout her daughter's house. Unlike my other Grandmother, Natasha who was very quiet; Moriah, or Mora as her husband called her, in my eyes, was a dramatic prayer warrior and practiced the uncommon prayer of wailing. Yes, I said wailing. It was quite a thing. Very real to her, it was understood by even my own mother, that this was an acceptable prayer practice.

When I was about 12 years old, I remember Baba Moriah visiting us in Max, North Dakota to see my dad. As soon as she got up, always dressed in a black blouse, black floor length skirt and black shoes, 5' 1" Moriah would get down on the floor onto her hands and knees, moving forward and backward, as if getting into a trance. As her hands lifted in praise, she would let out a howl that scared me as I ran out the door, terrified. I surely hoped, as she got our immediate attention, she would get God's and stop wailing. Today I look back at this and know with certainty she was in a trance. Although I still do not know why, she eerily kept this practice daily. Of course, my mother told us to not pay attention! If you can imagine, with Baba's guest room just off the kitchen, how could you not pay attention?

My Aunt Kate's husband, Al, was proud of his French heritage and if he spoke any language besides English, it was French. It is doubtful he would have even been interested in learning how to speak Russian or he would have in the 17 years Baba Moriah lived with them. But my husband heard stories from Al and Kate when he stayed with them as he got his work settled in San Diego before our arrival. He described their respect for each other as she lived out her days in San Diego. I can only imagine my Uncle Al being relieved of her daily rituals, but his good humor always served him well.

Many people may look at our journey and think we had overcome many milestones from the time we left North Dakota until we had parked our home in San Diego, but we did not see it that way. Thanking God was natural to us. But we were amazed to think about the seven months it took us to get here. My husband was even more amazed. As he rocked in his burgundy-colored rocker, he said he was grateful we were here, his family was home with him now. He recalled the radiator's replacement just after we left North Dakota, the trailer's flat tire and leaving the family on the dark highway in Wyoming; Donner's Pass experience; having no money for food and finding the $20 when we really needed it; the trailer park the family could stay in while he went to San Diego; the groceries left for us at Christmas; as every turn and every step there were miracles on our doorstep.

And now we were all together. God had delivered our dreams and desires – with more resolve to count our blessings than ever before, we were finally in San Diego.

Imperial Beach 1959

When you pass through the waters,
I will be with you; and
when you pass through the rivers,
they will not sweep over you....
Isaiah 43:2 (NIV)

Chapter 10

Imperial Beach 1959

After finding our new church the next order of business was to put the boys in school. Fred and Sam would be going to elementary school and Rod, Linda, James, and Del would-be home with me.

Clearly God has a sense of humor. It always amazed me throughout my marriage that Dutch did not know the breadth of the tasks I did to maintain our home. And to be sure it is amazing that many things did get done because women, unlike most men, multi-task. It is so easy to start one project, like hanging the clothes out to dry on the line, then walking past the discarded toys of the kids – only to know I had to organize them out of the pathway so no one injured themselves; then get distracted by a neighbor that wanted to chat; excuse myself to run off and see what the kids are doing left alone for 10 minutes; to at least 16 other chores that urgently needed my attention immediately while I waited for the clothes to dry so I could fold them and put them away before starting dinner. A half dozen diaper changes were also squeezed in while calming crying kids down. Calamity Jane had nothing on me.

It really is a wonder that things got completed! Given that same task Dutch would likely have taken the laundry to the line, hung it up and then gone back to his easy chair to take it easy, done for the day, assuming the clothes could just find themselves put away like a scene from Mary Poppins, while dinner magically appeared. I took it in stride and was grateful he provided me with the ability to stay home and raise the kids.

We put Fred and Sam in school at Lauderbach Elementary a few blocks away. We walked them to and from school every day until they knew their way home and had found friends a few doors down to walk with. It was a different and safer time. We did not worry that someone would snatch our kids and hold them for ransom, like Charles Lindbergh's child. As we had more children, however, we secretly joked that if someone really did take a child for ransom, we would have gotten a call to come get them. As they grew, I marveled at how much food they could consume. Our call would have been to pay us to take them back!

No picky eaters here. If you did not like what was on the dinner plate someone else volunteered to eat it. That can have a miraculous impact on the dinner protocol. As each child eyed their portion, and then the other's portions, I am still amazed I got them to close their eyes for dinner blessings to be said. Chicken legs were a hot commodity.

I still laugh at the joke a preacher told us one Sunday morning, about the 3-legged chicken. As the story goes a farmer bred a particular chicken to have 3 legs. A city clicker driving on the highway near the farmer's property was amazed to see a chicken running alongside his car, at the 40 MPH speed he was driving. Then in a flash he was passed by this 3-legged chicken. The chicken ran onto the farmer's property. Out of amazement and curiosity the city slicker followed the chicken onto the property and stopped when he saw the farmer. As he got out of his car the city slicker asked if the farmer had seen a three-legged chicken run past. The farmer slid back on his heels and smiled as his hands dropped into his overall pockets, and said, "Yup". With brows furled the city slicker asked if the chicken belonged to the farmer. Again, the farmer said, "Yup." The city slicker asked the farmer why he had a three-legged chicken. The farmer said, "Most folks like the chicken leg. In fact, a family of 3 can be rightly satisfied with one leg apiece. I bred this chicken to produce more chicken legs." "Well, how does it taste?" asked the city clicker. The farmer responded, "I do not know, I have not been able to catch him!"

The kids were no stranger to vegetables. A healthy portion of potatoes with chicken gravy, and an oversized portion of spinach went with whatever meat portion I served them. They were not fond of string beans, but an early childhood role model told them, "If I eats me spinach, I 'm strong to the finish, I'm Popeye the Sailor Man – toot too" They would sing this song while they happily ate their spinach, then off to bath and bed to end the day.

Fred and Sam initially seemed a little confused about the weather – during the previous summers they could go out and play. This was extended summer weather so, "Why are we going to school?" they would ask. Late summer still had plenty of sunshine and sometimes we would end the day at the beach. Weekends we frequently went there. When we went, we were often the only family there. There was not a lot of traffic in Chula Vista, our closest town. Weekly shopping was at the Food Basket, which later merged with Lucky Stores brand, at 3rd and J. Today a Sprouts stands where that original Food Basket was. My Aunt Kay and Uncle Al lived across the street from it and we frequently saw them shopping there.

We were located a few miles north of the US/Mexico border adjacent to the then Pacific Highway auto trail, which has since become the I-5 N/S freeway. Although the 1-5 freeway dates back to 1947, it was built in segments to provide a path from the most southern part of the United States beginning at the US border town of San Ysidro, to the northern Washington/Canadian border. That interstate replaced many of the auto trails from the Pacific Highway to the 99 freeway in central California and averages over 450,000 car counts a day in just Southern California Sometimes we would even venture to the beach across the Tijuana border. Then, we would drive across the border, barely slowing down. Coming back was just as easy. Occasionally we might slow down at the border, where we were stopped and asked what we bought or where we had been. On rare occasions we saw a car pulled over into a secondary inspection area with its trunk opened to show its contents. Even though we could not see who was in that car, we would gawk and stare at what was in the trunk.

Every day was such a nice day we found ourselves almost anticipating that some sort of weird weather pattern would instantly show up and make us scurry for cover, but fortunately that never came. The coldest winters, physically and figuratively, were behind us. But still, we were not quite sure what to think or expect in our second winter there. No snow boots, heavy gear, no additional expense for the car. Ok we got that in Redlands.

But how long could this last before a snow flurry or a thunderstorm was suddenly on us? Big thundery dark clouds with a clapping sound that always sent the kids under the covers or hiding their ears. But it did not come. Not then, not even in the sixty-five years I've lived here since. After growing up in the Midwest through the coldest winters in the United States, outside of Alaska, this new weather did something to our minds. Was I just imagining this or did the bread even rise differently – easier?

The kids got along well with each other. Fred was the boss, followed by his recruit, Linda. Sam did not care about rules and Rod would remind everyone that there would be consequences if they did not follow them. James followed the rules if someone was making sure he did. He was always checking things – opening the cabinet doors, everything pulled out from under the sink; pots and pans strewn across the floor. Fred, with his hands on his hips, would command James to put things away before Mom came in. Rod would remind him that he was going to get in trouble, as if that was an incentive to abruptly replace James's curiosity. When he did put things away, they were put back in a manner that he could find them. Sometimes it was better than my organization but often I was looking for something I knew should be in a specific place. Each one of the kids had specific and unique quirks and personalities that were emerging.

When we were not at the beach, weekends meant a trip to the zoo. It literally became our second home. Still today a few of the kids maintain an annual membership, attesting to the generational lasting of fond memories.

It was 1960, and when school was out for summer, we looked for and found our first home to buy – an investment home that included a rental unit. The kids were growing, and we needed more room. For a year as I drove through Palm City to the beach, I would often look at houses and imagine me living there. I would think about how I would decorate it, what color I would paint the bedrooms, what I would serve for Christmas dinner and how big a garden I could grow.

We bought a duplex at the corner of Emory and Coronado, which is Imperial Beach Blvd today. This odd little town called Imperial Beach had only incorporated itself a few years earlier in 1956. This was the same town I had gone through many times on my way to take the kids to the beach. It was a small, charming beach town with 4 miles of beachfront and, according to the 1960 census, had a population of 17,773. With non-existent crime this was a perfect environment to raise the kids in.

The mobile home we had lived in for five years, with a total of 450 livable sf, was used as a down payment for the duplex. Our realtor, Mr. Bean, arranged for our mobile home to be brought to the duplex, where the contents were ceremoniously emptied out before the mobile home was triumphantly driven off to a new owner. As I watched that home leaving my driveway there was a moment of silence and sadness for the memories and good times we'd had in that home. But now was not the time for sadness. Melancholy has its place - and there will always be plenty of time for it but right then I had work to do, and I was highly motivated with my team of eager beavers ready to help.

The moss green couch, clothes, toys, dishes, pictures, my husband's burgundy colored rocker, wagons, brooms, laundry – loads and loads of laundry; bedding were all brought into our new home. As we put our things in place, the kids ran from room to room, and all around the property. They had never experienced this much room and it felt like the yard was a park. I was grateful it had a fence around the property so the kids would not be tempted to run up the road. Coronado Avenue was still a graveled street and of course there were no sidewalks yet. But we had two bedrooms that seemed like a palace compared to our mobile home; a large bathroom and hardwood floors throughout. Dutch went to work opening the kitchen wall to the living room. We were ahead of our times back then as open living space is now considered a must. This created enough room for us to put in our first Formica table with shiny chrome legs. I was so proud of my new home. Immediately I thought of inviting my own family as well as my husband's family because we finally had room to put everyone.

That September Fred, Sam, Rod and Linda were enrolled at Imperial Beach Elementary School. It was a short several block walk of total adventure and surprise. Sam was mesmerized by the butterflies and Linda with the flowers. Sometimes Fred and Sam would race each other from block to block, waiting for the others to catch up. It was a happy time for our family. While the older kids were in school, I busied myself with planting a garden while the younger ones napped. I had posted the stakes with the seed packages so I could identify my vegetables from a weed in the fledgling garden. I hoped to have something to harvest before my mother and youngest sister, Donna, would arrive for their first California trip.

Dutch would not hear of anything else and insisted on giving my mom and sister our bedroom. Besides, it was far easier for me to monitor the kids and keep them from terrorizing their grandmother in the early hours. I am sure my mother would not have minded the kids jumping all over her, but I am also sure she was grateful they did not.

Mom marveled at the fall weather and helped me in the garden. She was a wizard at this and could grow anything. My young sister was growing up and would be heading for college soon. I could not wait to show them my little town and expand their horizons by taking them south of the border. Pictures prove their delight as they sat on a wagon, pulled by an alleged zebra – which was a painted donkey, as we all donned our very large sombreros in Tijuana.

We made our way up the strand, a seven-mile strip of paved road from Imperial Beach to Coronado, to walk the beautiful grounds of The Coronado Hotel. It was the largest resort in the United States when it was built in 1887 and was still the shining jewel of San Diego.

There was the military base, Ream Field, just a few blocks away, we wanted to but could not explore. Established in the World War I era, it was deactivated in 1944. Due to the Korean War, it became home to the first Helicopter Squadron in 1951 when HU-1's was brought in. It was then commissioned as the Air Station, Ream Field, having gone through many prior names. Surprisingly the Navy retained the designation, Ream Field, previously named for an Army Officer. But it became home to all helicopter squadrons of the Pacific Fleet. Leading up to the Vietnam War, the airfield was upgraded to a Naval Air Station (NAS). The end of the Vietnam war caused Ream Field to be disestablished and the facility became a landing field, ALF, again. Today it is still the home to all helicopter squadrons of the Pacific Fleet.

We had become used to it, but my mom and sister would lose count of all the helicopters that flew in and out of the air base. Sometimes there would be a squadron of helicopters that would rattle the dishes on the counter. If you can remember or imagine the movie "Apocalypse Now," and the accompanying sounds of Richard Wagner's "Flight of the Valkyries "you will have the imagery of what we saw every day in the air, just a few blocks away from us. That would be intensely intimidating to the enemy, but we felt secure and never thought of war or invasion of us. Who would? San Diego was a military town, and every branch of the service was well established and represented.

We visited Coronado and drove our car onto the ferry that took us across the Coronado Bay to the landing in downtown San Diego. We walked along the landing and looked at all the tuna fleet that was so abundant. A few times we saw a boat come in loaded with tuna as it laid lower in the water.

In his house are many mansions, if it were not so, I would have told you.

But of all the things I took my mother to see it was the garden growing that amazed her most. Although we wrote to each other weekly, and I had told her I was planting, she was a "see it to believe it" person and seeing that garden must have confirmed to her that I could take care of my family. She had previously told me she'd hoped I would have a home (probably so I would stop moving around.) I may have thought of this moving around as an adventure, but now understood how important this was to her and to my growing family. She probably had to know I could take care of my family and as a farmer, growing a garden was proof.

Since we did not have the modern convenience of a laundry facility provided by the mobile home park anymore, our first purchase was an old Montgomery Ward wringer washing machine. It was maybe two steps removed from washing clothes over a rock at a creek or beating the wet clothes with a plunger. It was quite a contraption and its two-piece configuration was downright dangerous.

The machine had a "safety" feature that popped the upper dual wringer in the event you got your hand caught, which apparently was frequent. This is probably why there are so many safety features today like seatbelts, clasps on wash machines; locks on doors of moving parts – as these hazards were common day occurrences we lived with. The wringer washing machine required you to take the sopping wet clothes from the lower tub, as it drained into one of the two concrete sinks, into the other sink filled with rinse water, then into the waiting and spinning wringer above. While you were feeding the clothes through the upper wringer to wring the water out (thus the name wringer washer) it would pop up if your arm accidentally got fed into it while hurriedly putting the wet clothes through. The machine was in the carport between the two units. The ringer, activated by a push bar, had two opposing rollers eagerly awaiting clothes to be fed into it to squeeze the water out.

In a game of chicken or dare Fred and Sam double dog dared each other to play with the activation bar. On more than one occasion one of the kids would run into the kitchen screaming that Fred or Sam's arm was caught in the wringer. As horrifying as this is to this day, I am grateful that the wringer did not do more damage than traumatize my young children. In fact, I am so grateful that God's mercy was always on us and watching over us. They could have broken a wrist or arm, or even dislocated their shoulders. And what if the wringer had malfunctioned and not released the wringer? In the mind of "what if," it was a miracle that my little angels came running to alert me and a bigger Angel of God protected those small children.

Dutch had work every day. Even though it was a lot of work with the kids I had the energy to be able to take care of them. I do not know what I would have done if I had had to take one or more of them to the hospital. I hardly knew people and what would my tenant think of me as a parent? These are things you think about as a young adult, that do not make a lot of sense in retrospect. I can only thank God for our daily blessings and that I needed to be more alert every day as my children grew and apparently grew in desire to challenge, dare, and defy each other as well as logic.

It was not long before Dutch's family, the Sniders, visited. My father-in-law, Roy Edward, "R.E.," wanted to bring out their old Plymouth station wagon to replace our aging green station wagon. We had been to a lot of Friday night drive-in movies in that green car. We would back up that 1948 wagon, with its hydramatic shift on the steering column, open up the back, and lay down two of the seats so all the kids could pile up and sit on their elbows, with their faces in their hands and watch movies. There was always a double feature, with cartoons at the beginning of the first movie. There would be a rush of all the movie goers to the concession stand between movies, but the kids ran to the swings until they saw the double flash at the bottom of the screens indicating the second feature was about to begin. They always fell asleep in the second feature and then we would head home. That car held 9 people, an omen of the future.

When the Snider's presented that car I tried to hide my lack of enthusiasm. It was more faded than the green station wagon. If it had been red, it had seen better days. It was smaller than the three-row green station wagon but R.E. thought he was bringing us a great gift. It even came with the left-over case of oil it used to get from Montana to Imperial Beach.

They also brought out "Old Steve". Steve was an old farmer that was known to Roy's family. Not much, if anything, was known about Alzheimer's then. But based on what is known today I can only surmise he would have been diagnosed with this. As he aged in the next few years his mental capacity worsened. He eventually died at RE and Beulah's home in Hot Springs Montana. But in 1960 he did some odd things. One comes to mind.

We had neighbors adjacent to us on Coronado Avenue, George, and Francis Conklin. George was a retired grocer and Francis was colorful in demeanor and style. They were in their late 60's early 70's. Steve paid them a visit, by knocking loudly on their door. When Francis answered the door in her plunging sweetheart neckline dress, small skinny heels, and pitch-black long hair she saw a disheveled Steve that offered his services to slop the hogs and feed the chickens. They may have seemed like characters out of misplaced movies to each other. He was bewildered and she must have thought of him as abstract. Thankfully George walked over to the house and told my husband, "I think this man belongs to you…. but there's a man at my house that wants to feed the chickens and pigs!" RE and Dutch went and retrieved Steve. When RE and Beulah boarded the train to go back home with Steve it may have been the last lucid moment he had. Steve lived another 6 years and retreated into his thoughts each day as my in-laws provided his care.

As we drove the new used car back from the train station, I wondered why we even sold our other car. This car had an area of the floorboard directly behind the front passenger seat that was rusted out. What kind of danger could this put the kids in? Could we fix it? Just as I thought about this, the front seat I was sitting in collapsed into the back seat. Oh boy, here we go.

Where Two Or More Are Gathered

For where two or three
are gathered together in
my name, there am I in
the midst of them.

Matthew 18:20 (KJV)

Chapter 11

Where Two or More are Gathered

After we moved into our new house, we made Midway Baptist Church our new spiritual home. It was only a few blocks away and was a highly active church for people of all ages. It was easy for me to make friends.

From the time I took a public speaking course in high school, I was able to make conversation with anyone. With thirteen kids in your high school class, it was like a private school and the teacher student ratio made it possible to get a lot of attention. Having eliminated the uhhhhhs, and mmmms, and having a clear idea on what I wanted to say, made it easy to communicate.

Everyone was so friendly and seemed to want to be involved with daily living activities that were woven seamlessly together. Every two or three months we would be invited to a church member's home. I find this particularly amazing because we had six small kids to feed by then. That we were invited at all was amazing. The town was friendly. Everyone knew your name. The ladies cooed over Del in the nursery, with his cute little dimples. Everyone helped us get the kids where they needed to be. The kids made friends with all the other kids that attended. The church represented a big part of our daily lives. We attended Sunday morning and evening services and Wednesday night choir practice and prayer meetings. Potluck dinners occurred once a month. Occasionally the church family would head out to the beach. We knew all the families, but we were close with 4 or 5. The kids went to vacation Bible school – something the church organized for a week or two in the summer – an early version of preschool I was grateful for.

The duplex we bought needed a lot of TLC. Much of the wood around the units had to be replaced, sanded, and painted. We didn't take vacations and opted to work on the house instead. When Dutch had a few days off he would start a project that would continue every other week until it was finished. He stuccoed the houses and what work he couldn't do he bartered for with a plumber or electrician to get the rest of the work done.

It was a time of great spiritual growth and the family flourished in our new church home. When the church at Castle Park sent the church transfer letter to Midway, they discovered I was a pianist and had played there at Castle Park. That transfer letter was like a resume, as they instantly asked me to play for the church and my husband to teach, as he had at Castle Park.

My musical training had started early when I was about seven years old. My mother knew I was a fast learner and could also play by ear. I played hymns and other songs until I broke my wrist when I was in the 4th grade. I was elated thinking I didn't have to practice anymore! My teacher said she couldn't teach a one-handed piano player. My mother was undaunted by this frank statement and found another teacher in Minot, thirty miles away, who taught the fundamentals of reading, playing scales and chords. I was never unprepared. Every week, until I left home, my mother drove me to and from those lessons. I played for everyone that needed a pianist, from choirs to weddings and school plays to plenty of funerals, making a whole $1.00 for some of these events.

Despite all the music training I was shy of the numerous requests for my services. It had been years since I had a piano at home so playing piano at the church was a welcome respite to not having one to play when I wanted. The demands of home were high and many requests to play for private events were welcomed as a musician but not as a busy mom of six, soon to be seven.

The church was an extension of our family and they eagerly helped as we welcomed a new boy, Dwayne, into our lives in the spring of 1960. We had announced to the kids earlier that we were expecting a new baby to join us. I would overhear them giggling and talking about how this new baby would come. "Would a stork bring it?" they wondered. I laughed to myself thinking of their double bed they had all slept in together, until I put in bunk beds. I never dreamed of having so many kids. After my first I thought, no more, and had tried to have my doctor consent to permanently shutting that department down. It was a different time, in Montana as it was in North Dakota and no physician would consider any type of birth control measure. In fact, I wanted to introduce all seven of my children to the doctor that suggested the rhythm method, who had five children to my two at that time.

Let's talk about this. Sometimes a blessing is hidden in your stark reality. I could no sooner send the kids back than the man in the moon, nor would I have wanted to after I held them for the first time. Holding children, having them hang onto you, dependent on you for culture, love, spiritual upbringing, are all things I embraced as a woman and as a parent. It was a gift from God, and I had been blessed with many gifts.

The simple upside was I didn't need to buy more clothes. The eldest wore their clothes till they outgrew them, handing them down to the next. And no child was in diapers past eighteen months, except Rod, which took two years and James, because of his cast. But as soon as that cast was off, he discarded the diapers.

Getting help was no problem. The kids were a great help, but the extended body of the church pitched in when I would ask for it. When I needed to hire help, it was $.50/HR, and I wasn't gone long. But it meant that I didn't have to have 6 and now 7 kids in the car going to the market. I could shop in peace and not be pleaded with to get

Twinkies, Ho-Hos or sugar-coated cereals. I think of how lucky I was in some ways that public safety didn't exist. Minivans were not available and if I had been required to put in child safety seats, I would have to have a car that was capable of buckling in at least 4 car seats, two mini seats, and all the gear required to carry with an outing. Our 1957 car did not have seat belts or headrests and I am grateful for the "mother seatbelt" which meant driving with my left, and right arm extended to those in the front seat, as if I could have held them back in a real emergency.

One of the ladies I met at Castle Park Baptist, Stella Tooker, had already raised her family and was a Godsend. There's no doubt in my mind God put her in my life. She and her husband had raised three boys and a girl. But her husband suddenly died, and she found herself alone. She had kept in touch with me. We had a phone by then and we would have short conversations to let her know how my family was doing. She may have been looking for a diversion to the sorrow and sadness one can feel when a mate suddenly leaves your life. All the things that made sense and gave order were gone. She insisted on taking over my household obligations when I went on my three-day vacation to the hospital to have Dwayne. And when I came home, she would come without schedule and let me sleep while I recuperated. She was a blessing that would show up repeatedly over the next few decades and I thank God for His mercy that we could both give something to each other we needed – her confidence and experience helped me get through the increasing challenges, and my reliance on her that gave her purpose; and for both of us the experience of fellowship of deep faith and shared belief.

That gift from R.E. was giving back in ways I had not anticipated. The car had to be towed a few times when we were stuck. Fortunately, Dutch was at home and could come up to the church a few blocks away, attach a large hook under the front bumper, wait for the long chain to become taut and be pulled home. I had to be alert. Even though the car engine wasn't on, I put the car in neutral and put the brakes on as we approached stops. Getting across Coronado as it got busier was more challenging. I had to slam on the brakes after we got across the street because we were at the corner of Emory and Coronado. So, I didn't venture out very far from home.

One afternoon I ran some errands and needed to go to the Food Basket in Chula Vista. Fred, Sam, Rod and Linda were in the back seat and the three youngest were at home with the babysitter. I started hearing the boys giggle and I could hear a clanging but scraping sound coming from under the car. "How was that possible?" I thought. I was on the newly opened little stretch of the I-5 freeway going north but I could hear this distinctive sound of metal on the road. I wondered if the muffler had fallen and was scraping along the highway. As people passed me, they were pointing to the car and I couldn't quite make out what they were saying, but knew it pertained to the persistent scraping sound I was hearing. One person rolled his window down and yelled," Hey lady, sparks are coming out from under your car!". When the boys heard this, they started giggling more. I asked them what they were doing. "Nothing" "No really, what are you doing?" More giggles, "Nothing Mom!" Nothing always meant something. I asked Rod and Linda what they were doing. "They're dragging the tow chain through the hole in the floor."

Leave it to the kids to find something to defy logic with. The under part of the car had rusted through but had been concealed with a floor mat the kids had removed. I rushed off the freeway counting my blessings I had something to do with my hands before I stopped and corrected this situation. The chain had hit the pavement of the freeway and as it dragged, let off sparks that the other motorists were trying to alert me to. I was really steamed up. When you're annoyed, it is hard to calm your emotions and I must admit the kids were now trying every edge of patience I still possessed. Kids don't understand logic or even danger. They understand love and when you are annoyed, in the

117

presence of danger, it is hard to be loving. I scolded the boys and told them the worst possible scenarios that could have happened but luckily didn't. They seemed to understand this and promised to never do it again. When they got out of the car, I remember kicking the car door real hard to close it. I was grateful to have a car, but did I really need one that had more challenges than seven kids presented? I don't know how I got through the shopping with these pranksters, but I counted on Rod to be the disciple of order and help keep them in line. If they got out of line, he would remind them he was watching and would tell Mom.

As the kids got older, they required more discipline and structure. One would cover for the other if it meant pardon for both. Punishments were swift but required more creativity. Initially putting someone in the corner was considered punishment, but it became a reprieve as I started to notice they enjoyed it and looked forward to it. So, I had to change out my methods of compliance. One would be assigned a chore and another the weed garden. When vegetables were harvested from the garden, they were prepared for the dinner meal. I was busy feeding the kids in shifts, so the older ones sat at the Formica table as I held Dwayne to feed him. I didn't realize it until our next move but apparently the kids did not like peas. Every time I served them, they protested saying they were gross and yucky. They were passing the peas to Linda, who always said, "I'll take them!" I wondered why she was eating so many peas, but the portions were not large, and I ignored her generosity thinking how wonderful the kids got along. I was just trying to get them to eat their vegetables with some variety. I later discovered Linda didn't eat her share of them either. They were passed to Linda, who sat next to one of the stainless-steel legs. She had pried off the top of one of the plastic sealants and fed the peas down one of the two tubes of the leg. When one leg filled up, she worked herself into another seat next to another leg, explaining she wanted to help one of the younger ones. She was helping them all right.

The kids had another babysitter, but she would frequently come over in the evenings unannounced about three times a week to make sure they had all gone to bed. Allie never had children of her own, so I was an anomaly to her with so many kids. She loved to see them all clean and cuddly – ready for bed. Me too. On most Fridays she babysat so Dutch, and I could have a date night. Sometimes that was only just a trip to Unimart, to shop, but we had our time together. The kids loved her, and she loved them right back.

This abruptly ended when the little Boston Terrier name Bobbie, given to us five months earlier, came out from under the bed, breaking the leash he was tethered to and bit Allie on the lower leg. She required over fifty stitches and many months of physical therapy. I was grateful we had home insurance to cover her costs for medical help. The dog was four or five years old and was very protective of the kids. Long-time friends Mabel and Lonnie had been unable to keep the dog because it constantly ran away. We had a yard and had consented to keeping the dog but after this incident worried the dog's tendencies might turn on one of the kids or one of their friends. We'd debated about whether to take the dog as much as we debated about having home insurance.

Work was good but money was still tight. The insurance and property tax were added to the mortgage payment making the insurance decision mandatory. But if we hadn't had insurance, I can't imagine how we would have paid for her medical expenses. We never said anything to Allie about coming as frequently as she did as the kids got ready for bed. The kids looked forward to her coming and would not settle down anticipating her arrival. Even after she left it would take a while for them to go to sleep. But after six months of therapy the spell of Allie was broken.

Poor Allie never babysat again. And Bobbie was sent back to Mabel and Lonnie. It wouldn't be long before the kids were crying for another dog, but we needed to take more time to select one. We didn't have to wait long before Dutch came home with another dog. This one was full grown but 3 or 4 times bigger than the Boston Terrier, Bobbie had been at 17 pounds.

One afternoon I put Del and Dwayne down for a nap and the rest of the kids were outside in the backyard playing. Del and Dwayne had developed a strong bond with each other and Del didn't mind laying down with Dwayne. Frequently what would happen though, was I would fall asleep too. A 20-minute nap can do wonders to lift your energy and spirits. I had just dozed off when one of the kids came running in yelling, "Mom, quick!" The alarm bells went off from deep inside my heart. This was different from the usual, "Mom! he's looking at me" or "Mom – he got more than I got" It was a persistent lower voice that repeated "Mom! Mom! Mom! Mom!" Like an alarm. We had only had the dog a few weeks. The dog was gentle, came with a 50 lb. bag of food and a doghouse that the kids would crawl into and share with him.

The gate had been opened, readying the dog for a walk and "Spook", the blue-eyed 80-pound Weimaraner, saw an opportunity to stretch his legs. The dog was always gentle but had a running spirit that was too much for a 6-year-old boy. When I came outside Rod had already been dragged a good 100 feet due to Spook's spirited excitement to get home.

But Rod never let go of that leash. He was determined to take that dog for a walk and bring him back as he had said he would. The profound character I saw in that small boy that day was demonstrated in everything he did throughout his life. Once he had an idea of what had to be done, he never let go. As I cleaned his scrapes and abrasions he quietly said, "Ouch".

I cried as my little boy's body was cleaned, revealing the numerous times he had been rolled over and over again as he hung on tightly to that leash. When Dutch got home, he was horrified as we all told him how this had happened. All the kids were talking simultaneously, adding to the hysteria of the moment. The thrill of a big dog was quickly dispelled. Although Rod was hailed a hero by the younger kids Fred and Sam taunted him saying, "…told you to let go!"

The next morning the kids went out to see the dog, as they did every morning, in Spook's doghouse. They ran back in and wanted to know where the dog ran off to. I explained that Spook needed a really big, big yard to run in and ours was too small. The dog had left with Dutch that morning, who had found a home for Spook with one of his friends the night before. A few days later I explained that their dad had spoken to the people that had him now and they were so happy because Spook was their big protector on their farm and would chase away the skunks and opossum. That was a lesson for all of us. Dogs given to us by well-meaning friends were no longer perceived as a gift. It was a gift that Rod hadn't suffered worse injuries. It would be seven years before we would venture into another pet.

Oneonta Elementary had just opened their doors. This brand-new school was a few blocks from the house and meant we didn't have to cross busy Coronado Avenue, which was becoming a thoroughfare of traffic coming from the beach enroute to the new section of the I-5 that had just opened. Palm Ave was wider and had a freeway entrance too, but Coronado Avenue didn't have any streetlights, and the cars were not impeded by the speed limit signs installed to slow the drivers down. That was a big concern to me and with Oneonta now open I was relieved.

With my small brood, one less danger we had to face was a blessing. The school made every attempt to make the kids feel welcome, including Saturday matinees. For $.25 you got cartoons, a movie and popcorn. I got a reprieve, as Fred, Sam, Rod, Linda, James, and Del ran to the school and were safely occupied for a 3.5-hour block of time. I would get the laundry done, house cleaned, and dinner prepped. I never worried about the kids coming back or dawdling or wandering off. If I said, "Come home after the movies," they did. They had a recollection that I would come and find them – wherever they were. For me, it was the only way to maintain order. That was important as the household grew - the kids were getting bigger and more independent, but I had to know where they were in case I had to pick them up or something happened.

The school was also a Godsend for the community help that we received. Although this program doesn't exist in today's school districts, the health program was robust and included a school nurse that was there every day to monitor the health of the students. The kids came home and said that a dentist trailer was going to come to the school parking lot and each of the kids were going to see a dentist. "Why do we need to?" they asked.

When I think of the nominal cost for the 3 fillings Linda got, two for Rod, 1 apiece for Sam, Fred, and James, I count my blessings. Dental insurance did not exist, but that health program was better than any insurance since, and included a yearly check up with a dentist, eye tests administered by the nurse and a call from her if the kids ran a temperature. And I got those calls. First to come get Fred, who had measles – then all of them. Although the kids had been vaccinated – it was mandatory not optional - they still got "three-day measles" and were all sent home to quarantine for two weeks.

Fridays meant shopping at Unimart with Dutch, and a babysitter for the kids. We found an older woman that lived locally and would sit with the kids for a few hours. We no longer had a dog to worry about, so what could go wrong, right? The kids loved Fridays too because it meant they got their "allowance". If the kids had done their assigned chores, and I was the final arbiter, Dutch would give Fred, Sam, Rod and Linda a quarter.

Since James had previously put his in his mouth Dutch was concerned about the risk of him swallowing it and changed the allowance to a dime. We picked up weekly supplies that included a box of oatmeal, 3 dozen eggs, 5 loaves of bread to supplement what I made, 3 chickens, a five-pound roast beef and 3 pounds of hamburger. As we loaded the cart, we would go to the produce section and pile on potatoes, and more vegetables that would be disguised in soup.

At that time, we were going through a loaf of bread a day – and the loaves were big with 20 or 25 slices. Lunch would consist of a PBJ sandwich with milk and a piece of fruit like an apple, orange, or banana. After the roast was prepared for a Sunday dinner, it would be repurposed into a stew or hash. Hamburger was easy – it was on the grill or in a macaroni. It would not be in spaghetti with meatballs. Even though the kids loved it they also loved playing with their food, and tomato sauce was hard to get out of their clothes. The kids made up their own reasons why they didn't get spaghetti – from the sibling jabs to choruses of,

On top of old Smokie, all covered with cheese.

I lost my poor meatballs when somebody sneezed.

They rolled off the table and onto the floor.

and kept on rolling – right out the front door"

Everything was used. Nothing was wasted. The freezer would yield whatever I had made a surplus of – or was tired of eating – to be used for a future meal. But it would be years before I would understand what the kids were doing with the vegetables they didn't like.

As we filled up the car and left, we would talk about what Dutch was working on, catch up on the latest family news, what the kids were doing, and his need to start his own business. He knew he needed to buy his own equipment, including a ¾ ton truck – and small business loans did not exist.

As we chatted away, I shared with Dutch that I was pregnant again. Our 8th. I thought I was 2 or 3 months along. By this time, I had substantial experience with this, so Dutch knew better not to question me with, "Are you sure?" With 7 and about-to-be 8 kids, we had to do something besides the methods that had already been tried but failed.

It was getting harder and harder to financially and physically support and now I asked him to permanently do something about it himself.

We were deeply absorbed in our own thoughts and conversation, and barely noticed the emergency vehicles approaching to race past us towards some emergency. But we pulled over and let it pass and watched as its lights and sirens disappeared in the night.

As we travelled towards our house, we saw some emergency lights and worried what poor neighbor might be having trouble. Before we turned onto Emory my heart leapt out of my body as I realized these vehicles were in front of our house! I panicked thinking maybe there was a fire.

Within seconds two police cruisers arrived with their lights flashing and sirens blaring. With all the lights flashing, thc kids spotted us and ran to tell us, "James swallowed his allowance! The fire trucks have to take him to the hospital!"

I ran into the house to see James, who was laughing and saying he swallowed a dime, and spotted the babysitter that looked like she was going to pass out or have a heart attack. "At least I have all the resources here," I thought.

I'm not sure if it was the panic on my face or the color of my skin, but the babysitter began apologizing profusely and tried to assure me that she didn't see him put his money in his mouth – and there were so many children to watch, and "oh my" at which point I may have tuned her out so I could focus on the situation as it unfolded. Fortunately, James's swallowing had cleared his airway, but that coin was going to have to come out. I knew how to child rear, but emergencies were not my forte.

For some reason, Dutch was totally calm and seemed to bring order to calamity. James was scooped up and put in the cruiser. That was a thrill ride for him, in retrospect, as Dutch followed this circus to the

Chula Vista Hospital, on F street, and I put the kids to bed, I wondered if I remembered to pay the babysitter.

What I Am & What I Do Is Who I Am, Or What?

Train up a child in the way he should go: and when he is old, he will not depart from it.

Proverbs 22:6 (KJV)

Chapter 12

What I Am & What I Do is Who I Am, or What?

Fortunately, the next several months were quiet – a calm before the storm. My pregnancy was uneventful. I had no idea if I was going to have a boy or a girl, but the ladies at the church thought they could accurately guess what I was having, by using old folklore and tying a wedding ring to a string. Since no one wanted to take their wedding bands off, they decided a dime would do because it was about the same weight. The string would be about an arms-length long and the dime taped to the string. It would be suspended by one of them over my unborn child. If it swung naturally back and forth it was a boy. And if it began to swing round in a circle it was a girl. This circle continued as I thought, "Wow, finally, another girl!".

Laurie Jean, who would later change her name to Lauren, was born November 25, 1961, a day before Dutch's 39th birthday. I was 30 and thought that I was too old to have children. My, how different things are today. My daughter, Linda, did not have her child until she was 41! My doctor's appointment, scheduled one day after Thanksgiving, informed me that I had two weeks to go before delivery. Laurie was born that same afternoon.

Man plans and God laughs. That beautiful little girl with the blonde curls smiled up at me from my arms, and I was in love all over again with another child. Bringing her home to the delight of the kids was exciting, but a special relationship with her older sister was bonded instantly. Linda hovered over the bassinet and was a mother's helper dream come true. She would hold that new baby every chance she got. If Laurie cried, Linda fetched a bottle. She had helped change diapers for Dwayne and was fully trained for Laurie. I was grateful all the kids helped but was especially grateful for the help with the infants. Dwayne was one- and- a- half, and Laurie was just a few days old.

With these many kids you need the help of everyone. Fred became the monitor, "Mom Laurie is crying" and sometimes would even hold her. The other boys would say, "I'm reading" or "I'm going outside" as they scattered outside. Chores had to be divided up, and Dutch would frequently take the older 4 boys, Fred, Sam, Rod and James, out on Saturdays for the day. The other four, Linda, Del, Dwayne, and Laurie stayed with me. Linda wanted to bake or make something while the others played or slept. When we were reunited the older boys would delightedly say they had popcorn or a hotdog and went to the zoo. Fred and Sam remembered the zoo in Minnesota and would sometimes compare what they saw that day at the San Diego Zoo, to their previous experience in Minnesota.

Our Brownie camera was constantly out and taking pictures, but I wanted something I could send to my whole family that commemorated our family in a remarkable but classic way and sought a photographer who would come to the house. Each child was photographed separately. When he wanted to pose Laurie with Linda, Linda had a little trouble hanging on to the now-wriggling little sister, and the photographer exchanged Laurie for one of Linda's dolls. We had an entire album that I have marveled at – mostly because the kids, instructed to stay clean for at least two hours, remained that way until the photo shoot was complete.

Weekends were always hectic. If there was not a movie at the elementary school to go to, there was the beach or a trip to the zoo, or just chores at the house. Sunday mornings always meant getting everyone ready for church. Our little 2-bedroom, 1 bath house was crowded, but efficient. It was easier to get the boys ready – shirt, pants, and shoes. The first one up was the best dressed.

A quick breakfast – Sunday was pancakes because we had a little extra time. Dutch flipped hotcakes and I scrambled the eggs, while Fred and Linda set the table. No one started without the other. It was not everyone for themselves. Teaching them the values we held high was important. Wait for the others – go find them if they were not at the table; help them wash up if they were not clean; say our prayers and be specific for what we were grateful for; all before they could dig into that tall stack of pancakes, as we heaped their plates with the goods. The boys would take turns in twos to clear the table and scrape the plates – as if there was anything left on them. Dutch would do the dishes as I finished getting ready, and we would all pile into the 1957 station wagon, Dutch had now christened the *Rush-in Car,* with 6 boys piled on top of each other in the back seat, and Linda holding Laurie in the front. No seatbelts for anyone.

A typical Sunday after breakfast, was church and the spiritual feeding of our minds and souls. It also meant the kids' social development was guided with the families who shared our same values. I could also relax my parental "second set of eyes," knowing the kids were cared for. I also enjoyed playing piano because it meant I could participate in the guiding of our musical direction, and from where I sat, keep an eye on the kids too. As the kids grew up, they shared their thoughts with me about a specific look I would give them. If I stared at one and that one was not watching, another would poke him and direct his attention to me. There is a lot of parenting you can do with a look. A raised eyebrow meant you were in trouble.

After church we had a lot of options. If I picked up a roast on Friday night, I would set it on a low heat before leaving and come back to the house smelling so good that all of us acted as if we had not eaten in a month, anticipating that Sunday dinner. Racing into the bedroom, the kids rushed to change their clothes from their Sunday best to play clothes. This also included the occasional disciplinary, "You do not hang your clothes up on the floor" instruction to hang their clothes up. About once a quarter we would have a family over, or we would go to their house. But Sunday dinners were a special privilege, and we took our time with that meal, to share what we had all been doing that week.

We also went out to a park in Lakeside where the kids could climb trees, run, or chase each other. The blanket would be set out for the toddlers to crawl or walk on before I set the picnic basket of things prepared the night before on it. Fried chicken was a favorite, along with PBJ sandwiches, and cookies. We also took a packet of the new and improved Kool-Aid that had added artificial sweeteners, eliminating the need to add a cup of sugar to two quarts of water and the Kool-Aid packet. This was less sticky and no mess, unless it got dropped, but it was definitely a Sunday treat since all other days they were served milk with meals. The kids' favorite flavors had memorable names like, Rootin-Tootin Raspberry, Goofy Grape or Very Berry. When the kids were called in for lunch, and saw me preparing the Kool Aid, they broke into the genius multi-generational jingle, "Kool Aid Kool Aid, Tastes Great! Kool Aid Kool Aid, Can't wait!" If you have ever thought, "why didn't I think of that" this is one that if I had been given a penny for, every time I heard it, it would have made me a millionaire before the kids were grown. They loved this, and a true testament to its appeal as a Sunday treat.

As summers ended, so did our outings, as we prepared for the new school year. It also meant the obligatory handing down of the previous year's clothes to the next boy, as they prepared to receive their new school year digs. This meant a new pair of high tops, four pairs of pants and matching shirts. If they grew too fast that year, the next one down got the new clothes a little early. Jeans were not in yet, and corduroy pants were a must. Socks, pencils, new lunch boxes with the latest fad on it, and notebooks filled out the shopping list, plus erasers in bulk that everyone shared, just in case someone made a mistake.

My status as a landlord was somewhat legendary. I remember seeing a lot of water pouring into the backyard coming from what I thought was the carport – the shared parking area between the two units. Thinking the kids were possibly playing another double-dog-dare-you game with the wringer washing machine, I fully expected to see them goofing off. As I rounded the corner, I expected to eye the boys in a stand-off with the agitating washer. Instead, to my surprise, I saw a copious amount of water being swept out the back door of the tenant. I suddenly asked, "What are you doing?" Betty seemed somewhat startled and simultaneously irritated at being interrupted from her routine. "What do you mean, what am I doing?" she asked, "I'm warshing the floor!" This southern belle was no stranger to a little spit and polish, but I could not understand what was causing so much water to be pushed out the back door, so I asked her, "How are you washing the floor?" "Like this," she said, as she picked up the pail of water and threw a bucketful across the kitchen floor and grabbed her broom, furiously sweeping the torrent of water, now being rushed out the back door. At that point I took over instruction on how to "warsh" a floor and protect my investment before it was swept out the back door too. Water can be very destructive to your property, and I worried about warping wood on the floor, or the door not closing, caused from Betty's rambunctious cleaning. She was fortunately willing to adapt to my cleaning method. But Betty had a temper and was not pleased.

I recall sending Linda over to return a spool of white thread. Linda was 8 or 9 and came back crying. She said Betty had furiously answered the door to her small, but persistent knocks on the door when Betty had not immediately answered. Possibly absorbed in something else on her mind, Betty must have seemed like a wild woman to this little girl, as she fiercely swung the door open, as she loudly growled, "What do you want?" as Linda timidly handed Betty the spool. "My mom told me to bring this back to you," as Betty howled, "Thank you!" and hurled the spool across the room and slammed the door. Betty was a one-of-a-kind neighbor. She was at once generous and kind-hearted, as she was quick to temper and terrifying. It took everything within me not to go "Mama Bear" on Betty, and I know I prayed for inner strength not to unleash my own protective swipes at her. Sometimes the calm reserve you are given, if you ask for it, can create the environment for remorse. Betty later came over and apologized for scaring and scarring Linda and regretted she had not been kinder. They moved shortly after.

John and Karen moved into this unit after Betty and her family went back to South Carolina. Karen was fashionable and John was dashing and good-looking. She wore her hair piled high on her head and looked like she had just come from the beauty shop all the time. Neither of them wore anything but freshly pressed clothes and had two boys who were styled after him. When I thought of them, I thought of the Good Housekeeping sign of approval. They looked like the perfect family. As I observed them, they observed us and how we lived too.

One day, Karen came over and expressed her amazement that we got everyone dressed up, ready, and went where she thought we were going to church every Sunday. I said," We always go to church every Sunday morning, altogether as a family after we have breakfast together." "How do you eat together with so many kids?" she asked. "We might have a lot of kids to feed but we all eat together unless they are in diapers!" I replied.

She commented, as many other families did, that our kids were very well-mannered and respectful. She wanted to know where we went to church and said she also wanted to go. Her questions began to include family values and rituals and were these things taught at church? I explained that the church body was an extension of our family, and that we shared many things in common, but most importantly, our love and worship of God and His Son, Jesus Christ. I explained that the rituals like making your bed as soon as you got up, getting dressed right after and before going to breakfast, washing your hands, and brushing your teeth, eating together, praying before a meal, and keeping order in the family, were more a family value, although some of this was shared at church, like praying before a meal and tithing.

"What's tithing?" she asked. "God provided for us, so a portion does not belong to us. Since it all came from God, we should return that portion so we can continue to be blessed."

Some of these rituals were from my childhood, like making the bed. Today, speeches are celebrated about this, lauding making your bed as an accomplishment – that if you accomplish nothing else for the day, you can come back to your made bed. It is that sense of orderliness that calms the mind and creates pride in the one thing you did right that day. My only child who did not ascribe to making the bed, also had problems getting out of it. Sam was reluctant to adapt my order, although he did not want anyone to touch the things on his top bunk. He could not understand why he needed to make the bed if he was just going to get back into it later in the day. It may have been his calculation to get out of the bed at the last possible moment, and hope that not being late for school would prevent him from having to adhere to the house rules. It was a constant battle though.

Tithing was always important to me. I may have been 16 years old when I heard my first sermon on tithing. Although my own mother did not believe in giving a 10% portion, Dutch and I began tithing a few years after we were married. In 1957, after Dutch accepted the Lord as his personal Savior, he made his commitment to God and to tithing. He never heard this type of sermon in the Presbyterian Church he had occasioned in Hot Springs, Montana, but the day he heard it in Minot he knew this was where his heart and soul belonged. It would be years, and until we got to Midway Baptist, that he would be baptized, but he never wavered in his commitment, including tithing.

By this time, the kids were ranging in age from the oldest at 10 years old to the youngest under 1. I still marvel at the energy I had to have possessed to keep up with the kids. As they grew, their energy and seemingly endless ways to antagonize each other did too, sometimes erupting in a spout of anger. One particular summer day stands out in my mind, as a reminder that as a parent you rarely have control, you only attempt to persuade your children into thinking you do. At least I think they thought I had control, because they would usually volunteer information about what one or the other and what they had done if I questioned them. Depending on how much fighting was going on, or unresolved anger with each other, one of them would bid up or down the wrongdoing, in a traded favor for mercy as the accomplice.

I had been looking for my new broom recently purchased. Since it was not in the house I came outside to see if I had left it in the carport. The 4 oldest, Fred, Sam, Rod, and Linda, were standing in the carport. Although this was not that unusual, the looks on their faces said it all. I had some experience as a parent under belt by then, and I always knew when the kids were up to something. Call it a Divine sixth sense, I would know if the kids had gotten into something or were about to. If one of them exaggerated the truth, I would ask them to look me in the eye and repeat that please. If they were truthful, they did not have a problem. If they were not truthful, especially Sam, would actually smile and say he could not say it. Fred would not look at me, and Rod would go stoically silent. Linda looked like she saw the whole thing, so I started with her. "What's going on?" "Nothing Mom, they chorused." Nothing always meant something, so I asked casually, "Has anyone seen the new broom?" Crickets. They were all silent. Maybe I was on to something. I asked each one. I thought maybe Sam had hidden it, but then Fred was acting funny. "Do you know where the broom is?" Everyone said no. "Did you see someone take it?" Fred and Sam said, "No! We did not see anything.' This went on for a while until I said, "Then you are all guilty!" All little soldiers in a line up, each protecting the other and loyally standing by each other, that if one went down, they were all going down. I announced, "As punishment you will not be getting dinner."

As they smelled the bread baking and the chicken on the counter, they looked at each other. Their faces drawn with disappointment they remained loyally, not saying a word. I knew they *all* knew what happened, but no one was willing to out the other. I am not sure if it was the fear of punishment or the guilt they were holding in, but to my absolute shock, Rod stepped forward with the announcement, "I broke the broom, Mom." I was totally speechless. He was the last one I would have expected to step forward. James, Sam, Fred? Maybe, but Rod? When I asked him where it was, he motioned to the opening under the house. I asked him to retrieve it and he brought me the two pieces of the broken broom. I sent them all in the house, all still uncertain if any of them would eat or just the guilty party.

At that moment I had to just walk and think about what had just happened. Each of them, not threatened or goaded by the other, had resolutely stood there and refused to confess who the guilty or accomplices were. I shared this with my husband later, who also could not believe how loyal these kids were to each other.

Everyone ate that evening, but this story stands out in my mind. It was not about the broom, it was about telling the truth for me, I explained at the table. My husband said, "You listen to your mother."

Again, Rod had been quiet, stepped forward from the line-up, and whispered, "I did it." Later that evening I took Rod into my bedroom and put my arms around him and thanked him for telling the truth. He never blamed anyone else when I asked if anyone else was involved. It was years before I would learn that Rod took a swing at Sam for relentlessly teasing and taunting him about Spook, who Rod still had scars from being dragged. The broom fortunately hit a wall, and not Sam, and broke in two. He was relieved that no one had to get punished.

Carrying guilt is a burden, even a small child comprehends. Carrying guilt about something we have done is also unnecessary. The gift of that moment was learning the unnecessary burden that is carried by not telling the truth. We all learned something that day.

Miracles Find You

Never stop praying. Be ready
for anything by praying and
being thankful.

Colossians 4:2 (ERV)

Chapter 13

Miracles Find You

The kids were now into a routine for school but when summer came there was always an adjustment, more for me since they were all at home at once. A schedule was a monumental task for the first week but soon everyone knew what they needed to do or where to be. Fred and Sam went to morning summer school. Rod went to the library at the school for summer reading club.

Dutch came home one Friday evening and announced he had brought someone with him to help unload the piano. "Piano?!" I exclaimed. "Where did you get a piano," I asked. "Your Aunt Lillian," he said, explaining "she sold it to me. She said I should buy you a piano and she had one, so I asked her if she would sell hers." I could never have dreamed of such a gift from my husband. It was unexpected and I wondered when they had had the time to talk with each other since I always knew who called the house. Maybe he had stopped by just to visit them, as he occasionally did.

But that day he just brimmed with pride in being able to make me so happy. I sat down and immediately started playing, ignoring the piano's need for a tuning. I was elated. I had often prayed for my own piano so I wouldn't have to go up to the church to practice or just be able to play when it suited me. God provides. I didn't care if we had to eat on the piano bench, I finally had my very own piano and I was ecstatic. But I made room. It was tight but since Dutch had opened the living room kitchen area into one main room you could move one thing this way and another that way till it fit.

It would not be long before I would take in piano students, producing a small supplement to the household income. Jim Knox came, then Gerry Golden, then Vickie Majors. That was sufficient. One student three days a week was how I started my piano studio. Jim was such an outstanding student. His mother, Florence beamed with pride as I said I was amazed that someone had self-taught themselves to the level he was at. It would be years later that Jim would in fact teach my own child, Linda, as she started her musical climb.

A member of the church, Bob Irwin, was also a realtor. He came to Dutch and told him about a house at the end of town…a house that was big enough to fit the family that had a lot of wide-open space that had just become available for rent. There were fields, for the kids run in and no surrounding development. When we looked at the house it was surrounded by fields of corn and alfalfa that was enclosed by rows of eucalyptus trees. I could imagine the kids swinging from a branch on an old tire and it reminded me of growing up in North Dakota. "But what will we do with our own house?" I asked Dutch. "We'll just rent it, just like the other unit," he said, "but we'll have to take it right away because someone else is looking at it. It's got a bunk house in the back and a double garage for my tools. It's the right size for us."

Dutch had gone on a fishing trip and thought he would be home by Monday, Labor Day, 1962 and we would move then. But I had gotten anxious about getting the kids to school following Labor Day and started the move as soon as he left on his trip Saturday morning. The boys were excited about getting to put their talent to use breaking something down. They pulled the beds apart, with some instruction from me, about storing each bolt and screw taped to the side of each of their beds.

Rod and Linda enjoyed putting the kitchen items into boxes – we had gone to Piggly Wiggly and emptied out their storeroom of every available box. James emptied out the linen closet. Next were the suitcases each of them had. They filled them to the brim and were instructed that whatever didn't fit in it didn't come with them and it would be donated. Each of their tiny hands were put to work, folding, refolding, bartering with the others if they had room for overflow in their suitcases. It was a joy to watch them because they each worked to figure out their own problems and then moved onto help the others with their tasks. We didn't have that much furniture. "How long could this take, I thought."

Remember there were no safety rules, about kids in the back of a pick-up truck or items being tied down to the truck. So, you can imagine the scene: Mattresses, box spring, beds, and boxes. Four kids in the back, hanging onto things to keep them from flying out and four in the front, two hanging onto or holding the other two. I carefully maneuvered the bulging truck slowly up Holly Street, after passing Oneonta Elementary, 8 short blocks to 1426- 15th Street. It turns out it is the last street in Imperial Beach, separating it from the City of San Diego, but still in the county of San Diego.

I did not recall how much work needed to be done when I first looked at the house. I may have been distracted by how much room there was and where would I put things that I had somehow overlooked the chocolate-colored kitchen cabinets with the diamond shaped black and white linoleum floors; or the turquoise-colored bathroom the kids would share. I had apparently skipped over the pink master bath and bedroom in my exuberance to not have to share a bathroom. But the house had hardwood floors that I would marvel over until dust bunnies relentlessly made it lose its luster after a few months.

The kids ran into the backyard and wanted to know who lived in the house in the backyard. I had to explain to them that there was a hobby and sewing room and a 2-car garage that their father would be able to finally have a place to store his tools. And we now had a covered garage that we could drive a car into if we wanted. But it would quickly be repurposed into a catch all place for the kids to play while we got the laundry done. As I unpacked a box, I looked out the window in the backyard and spotted all the kids over 5 in the pepper tree, centered in the yard.

Dutch came back early and arrived back at the old house on Sunday evening only to find that his family, and most of the furnishings, were gone. He came to the new house and was so amazed that we had moved. He said he brought help to move on Monday, but the only things left at the house was the stove, refrigerator, piano, a couch, and that wretched wringer washing machine. I secretly hoped it would fall off the back of the truck, but everything made it over to the new house.

Since we were renting that house, we only had the expense of moving since rent deposits did not exist or the realtor had somehow maneuvered past that conversation. But the house was barely habitable. It had to be painted and cleaned up. The yard did not have a fence and it was filled up with the previous tenant's leftovers they didn't take with them. The toilet was cracked and had to be replaced and plumbing had been a challenge for the two families that had occupied the house prior to us taking it. They had literally just left as we moved in.

We negotiated with the owner to do the work and take the expenses off the rent. We were grateful not to have to pay two rents, and until we could find a tenant for the Emory unit, sweat equity was our working capital. School started the day after Labor Day and we took Fred, Sam, Rod, Linda, James, and Del Jr. and enrolled them at Emory Elementary, leaving Dwayne and Laurie at home with me. Dwayne was toddling and Laurie was crawling, but both were easy to take care of. Fortunately, Dutch had taken the rest of the week off so we could get the house painted and in order.

At first, we thought 10 gallons of Navajo White would be enough to do the whole house, lightening it up from the dark colors. But we had not anticipated the dark pigments as we watched the pink, turquoise and chocolate brown bleed back through. All in all, it took three coats of paint to cover all the rooms. The piano was front and center in the living room and students began to find out about the studio from word of mouth. Initially, but then only on occasion, I ran an ad in the Star News stating I had opened a few time slots for new students.

We thought we were equally as fortunate to rent out our duplex after going back and cleaning it up. Although I do not remember the tenants name, they had 5 boys and stopped paying rent after the first month. This was worse than having no tenant at all because in addition to not paying for what they were using, they also beat the place up.

Even though I had cleaned and painted it prior to their occupancy it had to be cleaned and painted after we got them out. This meant we had to pay two rents. We could not afford the two places and made a partial payment, like we had done on my husband's truck a few years earlier, on the duplex. The money we made for the other unit was not enough to cover the mortgage, so we were short every month.

When we first came to California, we had the burden of relocating, finding work, a growing family, a truck payment, and a payment for our mobile home. Now we had the mortgage for the duplex, a larger family, rent for the new house, property taxes and insurance.

When we had gone late on the truck payments, when we first got to California, we tried to catch up, but as the song goes, "There's too much month at the end of the money!" and we could not keep up. Losing the truck was one thing but we had to do anything and everything, including cleaning the laundry common area of the trailer park to pay for the space rental, to keep a roof over our heads.

As hard a winter as it was in Minot, as Dutch hitchhiked to Fargo, we had already figured out how to work around having just one vehicle. In California we knew we could live without a truck but not a home. We had worked hard to get and keep the duplex. We always figured we would catch up on the payments and pay a late fee. When we finally got the tenant out in December 1961, we received a Notice of Default. Being faced with foreclosure on our hard-earned investment's financial gain, including the sale of the mobile home we had used for the down payment, was now at risk of all being lost.

Every month money got tighter and scarcer. In the 4th quarter of 1961, work was hit and miss as the US economy was struck by what is referred to now as the "Flash Crash", a period leading up to the Kennedy Slide of 1962.

We were not investors, but we were not watching the news or absorbing it if we had. We had plenty to think about already. But you do not have to believe in gravity to feel its effects. It had taken years to recover from the 1929 crash. But the economy had been experiencing a rapid expansion. Historically the GDP had risen significantly from 1951 to 1959. Stock prices had risen steadily since the late 1940s and our new president, John F. Kennedy had promised the recovery would continue.

But the stock market had another idea and suffered a massive decline. We did not understand the impact of panic selling but the S&P 500 had a 22% decline while the Dow Jones Average dropped over 5% in May – a one month drop- down almost 35% - the second largest decline then on record – giving it the reference of the "Flash Crash of 1962".

Recessions come and can take a long time to leave. In this instance we felt the impact in the little amount of work available to my husband, and the lower wages when he did have work, including jobs that were not even in his line of work. I remember him coming home and wreaking an odor I could not identify. When I asked him where he had worked that day, he said he had been shoveling chicken manure. It never occurred to either of us to ask for help, including government help. We never applied for or asked for welfare, public assistance, or government money. Word got around that Dutch had a truck and would work at most jobs except electrical or plumbing. So, he made steady work, just not a lot of money.

By this time, I also had students whose parents could not afford to pay for lessons but would barter or trade what they had for what we needed. One student's parents were farmers and brought eggs; another student's parents owned a rug company and traded a carpet for lessons. It was far easier to find work and more rewarding than to stand in a line waiting for a handout. This was a value we instilled in all the kids.

We were not expecting this news but in early February, the realtor informed us that the owner, who was living in Japan then, informed him that he wanted to sell. We were given one choice – buy or move. We had thirty days to decide what we were going to do.

Where were we going to get the money to buy the house? We were barely making ends meet. In fact, we were splitting at the financial seams, going late and short on the duplex every month that was now in foreclosure. This house was going to market in thirty days for $15,500.

We needed $2,000 for a down payment. The realtor suggested we go to the bank to borrow it. We would figure out how to get the closing costs of about $500 later. Dutch went to the Bank of America, where we were banking, and asked for a $2000 loan. Remember this was prior to computers and banking systems we are familiar with today. Without social media speed that is so common today, the status of the Emory house would take a few months to be recorded manually and make its way to publicly available information. But when the bank learned the loan was needed for the down payment for 15th Street they said, "No. There is no equity."

When he came home, Dutch said we needed to work our way down the list of possibilities. We had just paid the $500 back we had borrowed from my mother for the down payment on our mobile home, so I nipped the idea in the bud when Dutch suggested we draw from the same well again. I asked him about using his GI loan. Today that would be a VA Loan. He said he had used this to help his parents rebuild their home after theirs had burned down. So, I asked him if he would ask them if they could help us by loaning us the money we needed. Taking a loan out on their own house, his parents lent us the money as a personal loan. It was wired into our Bank of America account and attributed as a gift.

Now that we had a loan commitment for the down payment, we still needed to raise the closing costs of $500. But we knew we had to clean up our financial woes on the duplex or it would ruin our credit and any possibility of recovery through a foreclosure. Our realtor spoke to our private lender, Mr. Furlong, and explained that the balance we still owed, $13, 800 was higher than the market reflected on the then value of the duplex if you could even find a buyer. The market had clearly shifted. Again, we did not understand financial downturns, but we were in the middle of one as we watched our $2,500 equity, we put down on the duplex vanish. We would only be able to preserve our credit by gaining the cooperation of the lender as we quit-claimed it back to him.

Wanting to show our gratitude for the lender's willingness to take the duplex back, we went to clean and repair the unit the family with the five boys had occupied. After we painted, I began to clean. During my lunch break I looked through the mail I'd brought with me. As I glanced at the bills, I folded one envelope over the next, to the Christmas cards I received. I stopped at one personally addressed to me I recognized from my Uncle Joe. Every year since we left North Dakota he had sent me a $5 check for a turkey dinner. I held the envelope with fondness for my uncle's care and generosity and thought, "Well here is our Christmas dinner." I almost fell over as I rubbed my eyes in disbelief! The check was $500! Enough to cover the closing costs for our new home. In the card, he wrote, "I felt a strong need to send you a little extra this year."

God knows our every need. Even though I knew we would be provided for, I did not know how we would get the $500. Dutch was working hard trying to make the money, but he was a worrier. Without the benefit of a cell phone, I would have to wait for him to get home. I could hardly contain my excitement to tell him. But this news was not shared at the dinner table with the eight children. We always had a strong front and showed unity and faith at the table. We never discussed trouble or worries, believing this was not good for digestion. As the kids cleaned up, I went to the living room to talk with Dutch as he rocked in his chair. I said "Oh ye of little faith. If God provides for the birds and fowl, surely he will take care of us." "What do you mean," he asked, as I set the check on the coffee table next to him. I said, "If you have the faith of the mustard seed nothing is impossible. And I have that faith." He was stunned and stared at the check in disbelief.

When we went to our room that evening, we prayed and gave thanks. It was truly the first time I had seen my husband weep. With tears in his eyes, Dutch spoke of his gratitude for God's blessings and for his renewed faith in his belief that he was provided for.

With the down payment and $502.00 closing costs together, we could proceed to buy the house. With traditional mail services our written offer would be sent to Japan, where the owner was now living. A few small changes would be sent back to us a few weeks later. Our acceptance of those changes would be notarized and sent back to Mr. Forrester. His acceptance would be notarized at the American Embassy in Japan and sent back. This back and forth took a few months and we finally opened escrow in March. Our paperwork on the duplex was now reflected and our credit cleaned, meaning our loan would be approved.

We made monthly payments of $20.25 for the second mortgage, sometimes doubling up on our payments. But nothing would give me such great satisfaction as to pay that loan off in 1967.

Faith of a Mustard Seed

"And Jesus said unto them,
Because of your unbelief: for
verily I say unto you, If ye have
faith as a grain of mustard seed,
ye shall say unto this mountain,
Remove hence to yonder place, and
it shall remove, and nothing shall
be impossible unto you."

Matthew 17:20 (KJV)

Chapter 14

Faith of a Mustard Seed

Miracles of all miracles, we closed escrow on our loan May 24, 1963, three months after the arrival of our last and newest member of the family, Walter John. We now had nine children – seven boys and two girls. It was a miracle of all miracles in both instances.

The first miracle was getting a new house while we were in foreclosure and having no credit to our names. Yet we managed to get the closing costs miraculously handed to us from my uncle, secure a second mortgage from Dutch's parents for the down payment, and qualify for a first mortgage!

The second was truly miraculous. Despite Dutch's decision to permanently participate in planned parenthood (a vasectomy), we now had our final addition to our family, amen. Dutch quizzed me repeatedly, "How could that be? How could that be!" Walter was such a surprise because of the circumstances. And while Dutch pondered, I marveled at this and enjoyed what I knew would be my last pregnancy.

My faith never wavered. I knew God would provide for us. This was a theme throughout our marriage. But here is what I know about that. There will be times when one partner is stronger than the other. That belief we have in each other helps us weather tough decisions, hard times, or difficult situations.

The faith of a mustard seed – tiny in size – is a Matthew 17:20 parable. The lesson was not about a mustard seed, but about having a small portion of faith. Having the faith at least the size of a miniscule mustard seed, could result in something as incredible, but equal to, the ability to move mountains. So, it *is* about faith. The confidence and trust that I placed in God that my prayers and needs would be heard, and belief in God's ability to provide, was my faith. Faith is not about proof. Faith was substantiated by fact, though, and secured our miraculous new beginning.

As a result, our faith grew stronger and stronger as we continued to see more miracles unfolding before us. We need the memory of those miracles because they remind us of and help get us through the tough times. And tough times do not take long to show up. We would continue to marvel though, as work was becoming plentiful, and my piano studio doubled in size.

We began work on the house as we busied ourselves with making our home ours, past the initial emergency paint project when we first moved in. As my studio grew, students generally came in as school was letting out, and I would continue teaching up until the dinner hour. Fred was instrumental in helping to get the final food preparation to the table as he commandeered Rod or Linda to set the table, then herd everyone inside to the waiting meal. Those first few years on 15th Street were so busy that I chose not to teach piano during the summer, so we could continue to feather our nest and make it home.

Our kids were getting bigger, and the meals had become more challenging. Sitting around the 5-foot Formica table had been abandoned at Emory Street. After the discovery of all the crusty vegetables in the hollow chrome legs, I brought the picnic table into the house and covered it. To accommodate the family Dutch put an 8-foot sheet of plywood secured to the tabletop (no hollow legs here,) cutting "safety" angles on the edges, as if to hide the fact it was what it was. I covered the table with a beautiful sheet of orange Naugahyde material, stapled under the plywood sheet, and tucked the matching orange plastic chairs purchased at K-Mart under the table. The orange table and chairs offset the lovely avocado green refrigerator Dutch bought at a Sears parking lot sale. If there had been an orange one, he would have bought that too. He loved the color of orange. Thankfully, I steered him away from the orange shag carpet, opting for the brown one, until he got his way in 1974 with the burnt orange shorter shag. A few years later he would be in that same Sears parking lot sale and purchased, you guessed it, the matching avocado green stove!

Much like today we repurposed many of the items we purchased at the grocery store for something we needed at home. Dutch and I were solid coffee drinkers. Two cups each in the morning and sometimes a refresher pot in the evening, but mostly just early in the morning. We would purchase a one pound can that had a tin turnkey attached to the side of the can so you could open it. Think about how many opportunities you could have to injure yourself just to open the coffee can! Fortunately, we avoided cutting our fingers open with the sliver of metal peeled off the rim of the coffee can, as it was tightly wound around the coffee key that came with it. We would carefully open and close that can until we decided that was too dangerous and transferred the precious contents of the can into a sealable plastic container to retain the coffee's freshness.

Over the next few months Dutch came to realize that we could likely have another dog, as he came home with *Fifi*, the aptly named miniature black female French poodle. I was not so sure having another dog was a good idea, but she was cute and small, and sat in my lap. How can you not like dog who does that? Fifi adored my husband too, as she would jump into his lap when he came home, eagerly showering him with her kisses up his nose.

We kept Fifi's water bowl next to the stove until one of the kids knocked it over and broke it. We took one of the coffee cans and repurposed it for the dog bowl, but thought it was a better idea to put it in the garage. We carefully removed the top lid of the can and discarded it. The can was designed to expose another safety rim on the can that previously held the coffee. By this time, another manufacturer sold a plastic top to cover the can after it was opened, a true testament to its clear and present danger. But it had another design flaw. The can's safety rim was just pressed onto the top of the can and easily came off when the can was knocked over.

It was a fateful day in July that my husband's namesake, Delmer Jr., nicknamed Del, came running through the garage likely being pursued by one of his older brothers. He slipped on the water and fell on top of the repurposed but exposed rimless coffee can. He instantly cried, as my kids often did when fighting with each other, but this howl was different.

I was at the stove preparing the dinner meal and heard him scream for help. "Mom! Help! I'm bleeding!" "Well, come in and I'll put a band aid on it!" I said, as I wiped my hands on the kitchen towel. The door to the garage was adjacent to the stove, and as I turned and opened the door, my heart sank. I was horrified as I saw the massive amount of blood pooling where he was laying and knew it was something awful. I grabbed the closest towel and ran to him, as I yelled to Fred, "QUICK! DIAL 'O' and have the operator call the police" "Linda, get another towel, NOW!" I continued to apply pressure to his forearm that was severed at an angle from the wrist all the way up the forearm, exposing bones and spurting blood. When the blood soaked through the towel, I applied another towel, afraid to expose his arm. With this much blood loss I was afraid of his losing consciousness, or maybe mine, if I saw the carnage again. By this time, all the kids were surrounding me, and I was relieved to hear sirens as an emergency vehicle approached the house.

When the police officer got out of his car, he ran up the driveway and immediately reached for the side of the garage to brace himself for the gruesome scene he was viewing. Without hesitation, the officer instructed me to scoop my seven-year-old son up, and get into the back of the police car, as he made a tourniquet out of one of the towels and instructed me on how to apply more pressure safely. Without seat belts, police cages or computers, and armed with only a two-way radio the officer held in his hand, he urgently asked the dispatcher to direct him to the closest hospital, as we raced up the street with the sirens wailing. The Operator called the hospital, alerting them to the oncoming medical emergency.

When we reached the Chula Vista Hospital on "F" Street, fifteen minutes later, Delmer was weak but alive. We rushed into emergency, and he was quickly taken into surgery. Fifty-eight stiches and a blood transfusion later I quietly held my breath and waited for my husband. After surgery, the doctor came out and explained how severely severed Del Jr's arm was. "He may not be able to feel anything in his arm or be able to close his hand again," the doctor said, as my husband and I braced ourselves for what could possibly be next.

As I silently prayed, I thanked God for the miracle of speed, medicine, and the ability to get Delmer to the hospital without losing his life. That night, after we brought our injured little boy back home, everyone huddled around him. It was late before we got the rest of the kids to bed. Before we went to bed, we prayed. My husband, who was a man of few words, said, "You pray. I wouldn't even know what to say." There were times he had greater faith than I did but at this moment we held each other up in prayer as we gave thanks again and again for our miracle.

We pampered Delmer Jr. back to health, taking him back and forth to the doctor to change the dressing every other day. After two weeks, the doctor's confidence became ours as we watched the skin seal back up, lessening any chance of infection. The visual of that day has never left me, as I can still see that little boy laying helplessly on the floor, in my mind's eyes. While his small mind may not have ever thought of anything but getting his injury taken care of, I remember vividly praying to God and asking him to spare my child's life. I am also grateful that Del, as his calls himself now, is in his 6th decade of life and has full use of that scarred arm. He regained his ability to feel, use and open and close his hand, evidence of God's mercy.

It would be a few decades after this incident that he would learn his fate from that blood transfusion. Blood screening was not done in the 1960s. And it was not until 1985 that blood screening even began, a result of the then-worst communicable disease, AIDS and its related HIV diagnosis. It is now mandatory. But Del contracted Hepatitis C (HCV), believed to be a result of his blood transfusion. Screenings for this virus did not begin until 1991. An early diagnosis with the rashes he immediately developed, after his childhood injury, were overlooked because of his eczema. Two decades later, he developed severe symptoms, but was thankfully and successfully treated. God has clear plans for this warrior of life, which will become more evident as our lives evolved.

Dutch and I eagerly sought to put this horrible incident out of our minds and immediately began construction on converting the scene-of-the-accident-garage into something repurposed and more useful. Dutch's friend, John Pauly, a carpenter by trade, came and framed out the garage. Dutch enlisted the help of the boys as they lathed and plastered the garage. As much room as we had in our new home, the living room was a fulltime studio, and we needed this new space to live in. This became the new family room, as the partial wall in the garage was removed, joining the kitchen and family room together, separated by a counter and a step. Television, couch, and Dutch's desk replaced the tiptoe-walk through the living room, that was now cordoned off by a door between the living room and kitchen.

We never thought of ourselves as entrepreneurs, but clearly a home business and being self-employed are its tenets, and something we instilled in our offspring, as each of them have operated successfully as one.

As I recount this story, I could not have fathomed the near-death experience our young son had at the time. Nor could I see the foretelling of this incident to prepare me for things to come.

As we moved back into our schedule, we looked forward to the routine we had established. Sundays were always family church day, Sunday evenings we went back to church for Bible study. The young adults (think teenagers) hung out together in another building with adult supervision and guidance.

Going was not an option unless you were assigned an unsavory chore at home. But the social aspect of going was worthwhile to the kids. Monday was back to school. By Wednesday there was prayer meeting and choir rehearsal. The kids were volunteers to the choir, rather than prayer meetings with the elders. When I would occasionally join the elder's prayer group, I was lifted spiritually, as those prayer warriors brought the presence of God into this sanctuary of faith and belief. We prayed for those members suffering from an illness to someone overcoming a challenge. But the presence of God would carry us until we would meet again, and be able to renew or restore our zeal, that only a worship and fellowship can do. I knew the place for me was in my music ministry but those few times I joined the prayer meetings I was fully filled with the Holy Spirit of God.

There was never a dull moment in the house and there was always a lot of music. Not only did I have a full and robust piano studio, but by this time Linda was becoming a better student, studying with Barbara Bowers; Fred was studying violin and Sam had taken up trumpet. Dutch was active with something called Royal Rangers, an activity-based small-group church ministry for boys and young men, K-12. It was a leadership group to teach the next generation of men how to become leaders, not followers, with a mission and purpose for their lives. This meant that at least once a month the elder men in the church would organize an event like camping out, teaching how to pitch a tent, or start a campfire, and included how to pray. So once a month all our boys, except Walter, would go on these excursions.

In mid-fall of 1965, Walter was two and a half years old, and had developed a cold that did not seem to improve after the doctor's list of instructions. I wrapped him up and slept with him in the living room, where it was warmer and closer to the wall heater. He was clearly uncomfortable and cried because his coughing would wake him up. I slept next to him and had finally fallen asleep after he did. Dutch was getting up at 4 am to get to his Riverside work, when he woke me up and said Walter was not breathing. I leapt up in a panic and called the doctor. The doctor called the hospital who conveyed that I must run a hot shower, and stand in the shower with my little boy, letting the steam of the shower penetrate his lungs. If we were unable to clear his airway, we were instructed to bring him in.

With the memory of Del's life-threatening emergency so fresh, I was not about to take chances with Walter's health. I asked Dutch to wake Fred up and tell him he needed to get breakfast ready when the kids woke up, if we were not back by then. We rushed to Coronado hospital and the doctor was waiting for us and sped Walter off to a waiting hospital room. He came out and said we should just go home. I was not having it and asked Dutch to go home and make sure the kids got to school, with as much normalcy to the other eight that he could muster. I knew something was wrong. Call it Divine knowledge but that sixth sense a mother feels when she is getting information from another plane can only be sourced from the Divine. I called my friends at the church and got a prayer chain going.

Walter was immediately put into an oxygen tent and slipped into a coma. The doctors did a spinal tap on this fragile little boy to rule out spinal meningitis, and a series of blood tests were taken. It was not until the third day of Walter's admittance to the hospital, that the doctor broke the devastating news, that our last child may be breathing his last breaths of life.

He told us that Walter had a diagnosis of Hypogammaglobulinemia, complicated now by the onset of double pneumonia. The base illness caused a problem with his immune system, from the lack of ability to produce gamma globulins, or his immune system's ability to fight disease, even as simple as a common cold. Without this important element, his blood lacked the ability to produce the healthy red color of blood, and the ability to bring oxygen, needed to sustain his vital organs. As the nurses attached a life-boosting injection of gamma globulin, I watched it drip through his IV, and prayed for Walter's safe recovery, as he lay unconscious in his little oxygen tent.

Hours of the morning watched the light leave the room, as the onset of night came. I would not allow the possibility that Walter would die enter my mind. I could not. How could this little miracle dodge the most precise operation to prevent his arrival, only to be met with a short-lived life? This was unthinkable.

On the fourth day I was preparing to leave for the hospital, which did not allow visits until noon. The rest of the kids were in school, and as a passing thought, I picked up a small stack of pictures we had just gotten back from the drive-through Fotomat. As I sat with Walter, his eyes were open but there was no life coming through them. His soft blue open eyes had been replaced with a stare that was motionless. I moved closer to him and started holding up the pictures to him one by one. I said, "Do you know who this is?" as I explained who he was looking at. I continued to flash one picture slowly after another as I watched for anything to come from him.

Lost in my own thoughts, all at once, he startled me with "Hi Mom!" as a smile spread across his face, and light brightened his eyes in a fixed look at me. It was as if nothing had ever happened, and he had been there all along, just taking a nap.

The nurse, who had been changing a bag, standing at the IV, was so startled she ran out of the room, shouting to summon the doctor. As the doctor came in, the room filled with everyone from that wing. Every one of them would later say they had prayed for my little boy to survive and wondered if he would make it.

Everyone who experienced this Lazarus-like miracle of my son coming out of his coma, experienced the miracle I had been praying for, that all of us had prayed for. Sure, medicine restored his health, but the depletion of his gamma globulin levels, complicated with the double pneumonia, and the doctor's grim prognosis that Walter would not survive, the power of prayer proved the doctor wrong. That Walter survived is nothing short of a miracle. Wherever he had gone during his coma, he was now back. It would be a monthly injection for the next two years, but a small price to pay for the return of my baby boy.

To be perfectly honest I was terrified, scared and in total disbelief that Walter's life had been waiting in the wings between life and death. Just as I had experienced with Del Jr., that faith of a small mustard seed was my strength, and a reminder that our faith can and will carry us, and that we do not walk alone.

Never a Dull Moment

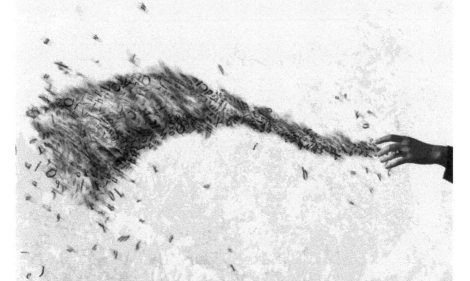

Trust in the Lord with all thine heart; and lean not unto thine own understanding. In all thy ways acknowledge him, and he shall direct thy paths.

Proverbs 3:5-6 (KJV)

Chapter 15

Never a Dull Moment

If you have ever wondered what a circus looks like behind the curtains, on any weekday morning you would have a bird's-eye view from my kitchen. In 1967, Fred was a Sophomore at Mar Vista High School, where he entered the 10th grade. Today high school is a 4-year experience, if you do not repeat a grade. Sam and Rod were in the 8th grade and Linda was in the 7th at Mar Vista Junior High. It would be years before the new junior high school would be reframed as a middle school and would include 6-8th grades. Back then, however James, Del, Dwayne, and Laurie were at Emory Elementary School, leaving the teachers to wonder when they would run out of Sniders.

Walter, now nicknamed Wally, would have one more year at home, which was fine with me. Despite the number of children, Wally felt like an only child. Not only did I know he was the last one, but he looked so different. Sam and Wally were both blonde and blue eyed.

The rest of the kids had brown eyes, until Linda's turned hazel. Keeping up with the kids was a fulltime job for four adults, let alone two. It was important to have order, discipline, structure, and responsibility, or there would be chaos. If the structure, responsibility, and discipline was not even-handedly done there would be anarchy. Keeping them busy was an art. But occasionally that energy could be challenged.

The church we were attending was planning a total church campout at Hume Lake. Hume Lake is home to one of the largest operated Christian Camps and conference centers in the world. It operates youth, family, and adult camps in several locations. Today it hosts more than a million visitors a year. There, in nature, we could congregate with other like-minded believers, celebrating Bible teachings and worshipping. Housing our family in one of the dorms was totally out of the question. Our family of eleven would fill the dorm of course, but none of us wanted to share or live in a one room-dorm. We lived in a dorm under normal circumstances, so this was a dilemma. In the end not everyone could go. Dutch had too much work, and because it was seasonal, he had to stay back. Staying in the dorms was not free but camping out was. Dutch bought us a tent and showed us how to pitch it. With a new Coleman lantern and stove, some provisions and a lot of spirit Fred, Sam, Rod, Linda, James, and Del we set out on a camping trip in the 1957 Plymouth's replacement, my husband's Chevrolet truck, with a shell on the back to house the kids and our gear. Dwayne, Laurie and Walter stayed behind with one of my good church friends, Joanne Hewitt.

The kids sang camp songs and played games all the way up the I-5, over Grapevine, and on up Highway 99. Arriving in the late afternoon we pitched the tent, and the kids ran off to the lake as I prepared our first meal. By the time Fred and Sam came back, Fred was itching. Nothing seemed to settle his itch down without being rubbed down with Calamine lotion, which a neighboring camper happened to have. That is when we learned the lake had a fungus that year, and foam had developed on the surface of different parts of the lake. The signs posted around the lake confirmed the fungus but was alleged to be safe to swim on. Swim yes, but not without consequences. That was not the only consequence I would learn about on that trip. We would join the churches gathered for morning worship after our pancakes and eggs breakfasts and enjoy the church activities until lunch. We would break for lunch and gather again at 2pm until 4 for the last of the day's activities and break for dinner.

It was during the dinner break, on the second day, I spotted a man and woman doing something that would have unintended consequences. After the kids had eaten, they ran down to skip rocks on the lake as I cleaned up camp. I happened to be glancing out into the beautiful forest, as my eyes stopped suddenly on the movement, and recognition of, someone from my own church. I stared in total disbelief. Here was the head of our church, respected leader, and minister deeply engaged in an unspeakable act with another member of our congregation. Neither intended to be seen or their act to be witnessed by a church member.

Apparently, my eyes were not the only set to see the inappropriate act. Sprinting from a nearby campsite, a young man also witnessing their act, ran to tell the pastor's wife. Little should be left to your imagination. I was so shocked and wished I could unsee what I had seen, but you know that is not possible. Without a word, I started to pack up. When the kids came back, I said we needed to get home and we would be breaking camp early in the morning. After their protests died down, they packed what little they had and got ready for bed and an early departure.

All the way down the hill, over the Grapevine, down the I-5, literally all the way back home. I watched in my rear-view mirror, as the minister followed me to San Diego. When we finally spoke, I just simply said, "Stop following me." I went home, told my husband, and avowed we would not go back to that church.

When a church body is sick, it can be healed if it seeks the redemption of God. Without that, it will continue to falter, as it did. One member left after another, and the youth group totally disappeared. When a new pastor replaced the old one, he had his job cut out. The church property was sold, and another property selected, that would include a school. This would slowly rebuild the foundation for the families to bring back community to the church again. Within a few years, it would begin to thrive and flourish and today stands as a beacon of faith, community, and strong leadership.

This was a good time for me to take a break. Although my husband and I were both active in our church, taking a break to restore my own confidence and faith was needed. Sometimes we need to do this in order to reset. That can happen in business relationships as much as it can happen in the church relationship. Resetting allowed me to pause for thought and acknowledgement to my moral convictions.

Summers began to change for the boys and their dad. Going to the zoo or the beach every weekend became more infrequent as Dutch's business changed. His work became more demanding making less playtime available for the boys. He told them they could come on the jobsite, and learn or apprentice what he did, or stay home. That seemed a better option than cleaning house, mowing the lawn, or other chores I would have created for them. My Saturdays were already filled with piano students, so everyone had to pitch in. As their skills improved, their allowance did too. They were rewarded with better pay checks as their skillsets improved. Initially Fred and Sam were the only boys who were interested. They were 12 and 13 when they started doing job clean-up and busy work with their dad. Rod was not the least bit interested. He said it was hard work and would rather increase his hours studying, at least until he was old enough to get a job at 15-1/2. James wanted to go with the other boys but had to wait until he was 12 before my husband would let him come. During the summer he picked up where Fred and Sam had started. They continued to labor with their dad for about 5 weeks in the summertime. Just about every year after Hume Lake, there was a vacation, and everyone was loaded into the back of the pickup.

That summer our neighbors across the street, Elsie, and Steve, would talk to us about their church, repeatedly inviting us. I was busy with the piano studio, the kids, and had a full plate. Eventually we relented, and after a few visits, became active members of Calvary

Baptist. It is in a small unincorporated part of San Diego, in a town called Nestor, on Leon and Hollister. The US-Mexico border is less than a quarter of a mile from the church, and this rural community was home to horse farms and large estates.

Nestor was named after a California assemblyman, Nestor Young. He served in congress from 1884-1886 and became San Diego's Harbormaster in 1889. Although Nestor began as a farming community of Japanese Americans, over time it would give way to the bucolic pastures and horse paddocks. Today many of those horse farms still exist and is now home to over 15 top organic farms.

We decided to take a little time off and go to Montana to visit Dutch's family. As the kids had gotten older, they assumed more responsibility of the younger ones. With so many kids, we had to devise a way of making sure everyone was counted so no one was left behind. There were 3 captains, Fred, Rod and Linda. Each of them was assigned two younger siblings, for a total of 9 kids. They assigned numbers to each other and would count off up to 9 when they were asked to. After a few stops we relied on them to monitor themselves. We would say, "Everyone in?" They would respond "Yes," and off we went.

We had been traveling for two days and on the second day we stopped in a park in Plains, Montana, twenty-five miles from our destination. We got out, ate, stretched, and played, then loaded back up. We began our counting system, verified everyone was in, and headed to Hot Springs. When we arrived my mother-in-law asked, "Where's the little feller?" referring to Wally. I said, "Oh, he's here..." "No," she said, "He didn't get out of the truck." With a doubt, a panic struck me with a dreaded fear that our little boy, who had already had a tough start in life, was going to continue that struggle. My father-in-law called the state troopers, and within minutes verified that Wally had been found in the park, where we had been, chasing birds. *No one left behind* became my motto long before the military adapted it, thereafter.

We drove back and got Walter and picked up where we had left off on this vacation. The kids were content to find rocks to throw in the creek, explore the barn on the adjacent property, or walk down to the Hot Springs swimming pool. We had been there two or three days when Dutch and I went with R.E. to town to pick up the mail and go to the store. In the meantime, Rod and Sam were in their grandparent's bedroom. They summoned Fred and Linda to examine a shotgun R.E. kept next to the bed that Sam had found.

Without hesitation, Sam picked it up and pointed it at Rod, who was a few feet away from him. Rod snapped and said, "Don't point that thing at me! It could be loaded!" pushing the barrel of the gun away from him towards the floor. Sam laughed, and said, "Don't be such a wimp! It's not loaded…" With that he pointed it up to the ceiling and pulled the trigger. Kaboom! Sam immediately dropped the gun on the bed, as the other three stared in disbelief. Granny Snider came running in, wet hands in towel, with a wild look in her eyes. "What happened?" she demanded. Sam explained, Rod interrupted, Fred paced, and Linda filled in a few of Sam's missing details. As Granny looked up at the sizable hole that had been blown through the ceiling, revealing the blue sky above, she said, "You'd better get busy and repair that before your dad gets back. She did not mention what I would do to them, but they knew they had just witnessed a near-death experience. Rod had always had a healthy distrust of Sam, but after that incident, he never trusted Sam again.

When we got back to San Diego, we immersed ourselves in the new school year and church. The new church body was a real blessing. There was a fairly good number of youth and made this an easy decision to get the kids all active and looking forward to their activities and socializing, with supervision of course!

Fred and Rod were both active in track and field at school and found fellow track members, Marty and Tim Hauck, Bob, and Gary Bell, aka the Bell twins, with their sister Donna, members of the church.

They occasionally brought other members of the team, including Jerry Jamison and Mike Cates. One weekend I took as many kids as possible from the youth group that could fit into the camper up to Anaheim for a trip to Disneyland. Martha and Donna Herdt, Suzie and Vickie Carpenter, Susan Clemens, Julie and Tim Tutwiler, Pam Marinello, all piled into the back with my oldest 5, Fred, Sam, Rodney, Linda and James. Friendships began and endeared to this day.

Over time, every Friday and Saturday night the kids went somewhere with this group. Sometimes those kids brought other kids. Soon word got out that these kids were having fun! Other youth groups defected to join those at Calvary Baptist. The Montgomery family with 6 kids of their own joined. Mark and Connie Montgomery often led music activities and would cart as many that would fit in their station wagon to the Saturday night activities with the Youth for Christ rallies in San Diego. Then the Bradley family, with Jackie, Beth, Nancy and Tommy. The Hinkle family, Shirley, Theresa, Pat and John came. Lori and Rene Green were followed by Larry and Paul Roberts, then Vicky Carter, Dave and Paul Hoover, Terry and Lynn Bush, then Penny Aaron came. And they just kept coming. As close as we were to Ream Field, the military guys found a new church body with the arrival of Ivan Berwager and Ed Rice and more.

When Sam was in the 9th grade and Fred in the 10th, we decided that the 7 boys, ranging from 3 to 15 years old in the same bedroom, no longer worked. They were fighting and challenging each other as the older boys picked on the younger ones. James was exactly in the middle of each group of the older and younger 4 and got the brunt of Fred and Sam's antagonism, which became progressively more aggressive. To keep peace, we let Fred and Sam move their base camp to the activities room, next to the garage in the back. I had readied that room for sewing and other activities for my mom's visit when she would come out. Fred and Sam were responsible enough to not be supervised in the back, or so I thought.

As careful as you are, and want to be, in guiding the footsteps of your children, they still have their own free will, and their footsteps can take them somewhere else. Sam was an enigma to me and quite an instigator. As charming and quiet and unassuming as he was, he was clever as a fox and fooled me many times over again. Fred was more transparent, and I could always get the truth from him, although not always voluntarily. When I thought they were sleeping they were out with friends whom I considered to be bad influences. The friends were experimenting with marijuana, and I did not want them doing the same thing. Despite all the church and family activities to keep them busy, something was still wrong because they wanted something else. When I felt those footsteps were on the wrong path, we needed help. I asked my brother Jim and his now deceased wife Joan, in Alabama, if Fred could spend a school year with them. Some one-on-ones would influence Fred in a positive way and Jim and Joan agreed. Fred packed his bags, and violin, and headed for Alabama in his junior year. His lessons paid off as he began playing in the junior orchestra, got his first job at Burger King, and made good grades throughout the school year. As hard as that decision was to make, it was a success in thwarting the friendship I believed was a bad influence. Sam was moved back into the house, on the pull-out couch in the den/office, off the kitchen and the back house was closed again.

Other changes had to be made too. The house now had 5 teenagers, all at once, to contend with. As teenagers, they are old enough to test their independence, but too young to do it on their own. Fred and Sam stuck together. Rodney and Linda were best friends. But James was the odd man out, being literally a middle child of two distinct sets of kids. All the kids before and after him played instruments, but not him. He wanted nothing of a sort to practice. As soon as he was able, James eagerly went to work with his dad and brothers. When James was 12, over the course of the next 3-1/2 years he worked summers with his dad, as their relationship eroded. James's behavior was out of the family's character. What we thought was wrong, he thought was ok.

And no matter what consequence James would bear from his misdeeds, he deliberately continued to defy his dad, continuing to test his dad's patience, until it finally broke. When the patience ran out, they clashed to the point where it had become dangerous.

Personalities and territorial disputes also began to become an everyday event, whether it was at home or on a job site. As mundane as getting up in the morning was, it had become a battleground amongst the boys. The first one up was the best dressed since they were all about the same size by this time, but the egos and testosterone levels were challenging.

Sam had also begun fighting with his dad on the job site and Dutch had his hands full trying to keep his business together, teach his boys a trade, and not lose his mind. Thank God Fred was away for the year. Although he would not have caused trouble, he certainly did not need to be there to referee.

Sometimes it is easier to send your child to the teacher rather than you trying to teach them. I had already learned this lesson with my headstrong Linda. Not only did she say she would be a better piano player than me, but also a better musician! Good! No problem! Do it. I sent her to Barbara Bowers for organ lessons, and I took Barbara's two children in exchange.

But where do you send a boy for a specialized trade and get his general diploma too without going to military school?

James's challenge was different. The breakdown was from a total clash in family values. Values are what you teach and demonstrate to your kids that you want them to emulate. In part, James was compliant. Mostly though, it was the small things that became monumental, and fights were mythically epic with his dad. I could not step in. There are some things that are between the man you love and the boys you want to grow up. Stepping in would have overstepped my boundaries and undermined my husband.

At some point, though, I had no choice but to, because if I had not, the authorities would have. When you reach this point there is no turning back. The ugliness and rawness had mortally wounded their relationship. When James asked if he could quit school, I asked him what he would do. He told me he had an opportunity to go work the trade and finish school if he left with John's family, to Colorado, for a couple of years. John and his family were known to us. On several occasions John H worked with Dutch and James got to know and like him. As a parent you cannot imagine the burden of feeling like you have failed a child. But we shared the burden that we did with James, through prayer and our support of each other for many years, prior to making this decision.

One member can tear the entire family apart and he was squarely in the middle of it. Every correction we made failed. The more we tried to instill our values, the farther he got away from us. My husband was a man of few words but together, as painful as this was, we agreed to let him go.

Initially James and John H. got along. John had a son with cystic fibrosis, and had expressed envy of Dutch, a man with so many healthy boys. John eagerly sought James' emancipation, which we would not give. James went with our blessings to Colorado, until just before his 18th birthday, when he arrived home a few days earlier to sign his enlistment papers and joined the army.

Fred had saved all his earnings from his junior school year away and when he got back to San Diego, immediately wanted a car to get a job. To make sure he would get one he applied for and got a summer job at Farrell's Ice Cream parlor 4 nights a week. It only took a week of driving him the five miles there and picking him up at the end of his shift, that Dutch and I decided indeed, he needed a car! Fred bought a 1956 Buick from the Herman and Freida Herdt, church members, for $100. It was big enough to put all his friends, his brother Sam and of course his little sister, Linda, who tagged along on as many outings as she was allowed. Sam always called shotgun.

Farrell's was designed to be a replica of an 1800's ice cream parlor. You would have to use your imagination that ice cream was served in an aptly named trough, full of 10 scoops of different flavored ice creams, topped with chocolate, pineapple and strawberry syrups, nuts, whipped cream and a cherry on top. It was delivered by two very eager runners carrying this vat of sugar-laden delectable dessert on wood rails, reminiscent of an 1800s fire brigade. To complete this scene, alarms were sounded to announce to the eagerly watching crowd something was happening. Kathy's Pink Surprise was my favorite…vanilla ice cream, topped with strawberries, whipped cream, nuts and of course a cherry on top.

As the kids got older the oldest 4 became more and more independent. Sam began working for one of the local carpenters, learning a trade at an early age, and doing odd jobs for residents. Since his older brother had a car, he also began to lobby for one. Besides, he did not want to ask his parents if he could borrow their car to take a girl out for a date he had been seeing at the church. Pam M. was frequently at the house and would sit with Sam and Rod in the family room talking. But Sam's interest waned as his interest in Julie Tutwiler, another member of the church, became apparent. With the kids so close in age, for a short period, Rod took Sam's interest in Pam. Fortunately, dating was mostly done as activities within the youth group, which had grown to about 50 by this time. One of those outings ended when Fred hit the meridian railing on the highway

It was a minor accident for Fred's heavy car, but his first bill arrived from the State of California Highways, as he had to pay for this damage. Fortunately, no one was hurt.

Ivan, another church member, had a seriously old Studebaker that always seemed to need fixing or tinkering. Our driveway was a frequent stop for the kids and their cars because it was flat. Gary and Bob, Ivan and Ed would stop and tinker or repair. Sam had his eye on that car but may have been itching for a car so badly that he talked brother Rod into going in on the purchase of an old Volvo from the Howard twin's parents. The first thing Sam did was raise the back end of that car and put decals on the differential. There were a lot of arguments between Rod and Sam about 50/50 usage though.

Rod took work at a local grocery store. Between that, school studies, his track and field activities and the youth group he kept busy. Linda was a little more enterprising. She babysat, ironed shirts for $.10 apiece, mowed lawns for members of the church, and was hired as organist at the Lutheran church when she was 14. All of them were enterprising and off to an independent start. The younger 4 were too young to participate with the older 4 and a division due to age became apparent. The house was constantly buzzing and was busier than an airport terminal, with all the arrivals and departures.

To say we were active in the church is an understatement. When Sunday evening services were over the fellowship often continued in our living room as the kids continued to enjoy their camaraderie and pranks. The multi denominational organization, Youth for Christ, led by Ken Overstreet, met on Saturdays and built program loyalty by structuring local chapters of Campus Life, hosted in the homes of local church members.

Of course, I volunteered to host this with my co-host, Freida Herdt. The program was structured with song, humor, and message. Food generally drew the kids in. It was probably one of these events that somehow Linda and Martha Herdt hit it off. They had the same humor and often thought up pranks that the kids would never forget. I am not sure who thought of what, but what one did not think of, the other one did. Their motto was, "Deny, Deny, Deny. Even if caught red-handed, Deny."

Martha would pick Linda up on Tuesdays and go to the Chula Vista library while I taught late lessons. They said they were studying,

170

but soon I got calls from various church members that female pranksters were calling and hanging up on them, then calling back and singing of all things, "Bringing in The Sheaves", an old American Gospel Song. What was remarkable was that these pranksters sang all four verses from a phone booth, and even more remarkable that the same church member listened to all four verses. At the end of this giggling escapade she would say, "That was nice girls." And hang up. They quickly advanced their pranks to include shaving son Sam's leg while he was asleep. He was a hairy but deep sleeper. With one leg out of his blanket they used electric shears to shave him smooth on just one leg, something he would not discover until the next morning in gym class. To retaliate, he knew Martha came over on Tuesdays. While she was in the house, he let out the air of all four tires of her Corvair. When she and Linda came out, they realized they had been pranked. Without losing a beat Linda went wailing to her dad, who had a soft spot for the apple of his eye. He made Sam go back out and use the same bicycle tire pump Sam had left next to the flat tires, to put enough air in the tires to get them to the gas station, and of course, onto their next prank.

When the Campus Life evenings would end it was Martha and Linda who would 'encourage' the others to go out and do something fun or goofy. This led to seeing how many people you could stuff in a phone booth – remember those? Clark Kent was not the only one to use those!

However, their pranks *could* go too far. They would not have thought so of course, but I recall one Sunday morning at church. Reverend Gates was giving his sermon after the choir sang their inspirational devotional piece. Linda would often leave the organ bench and join the choir and remain there until after the sermon, sitting next to Martha. I was sitting at the piano bench and noticed that Reverend Gates kept swiping at one of his very long earlobes. Then I noticed a congregant quietly giggling in the third pew from the front and looking directly at Martha and Linda. I began to watch them. They would stifle a giggle, then the earlobe would be swatted at. It was the small stream of water that caught my eye that I realized one of them had a small squirt gun and was shooting at the minister's earlobe while he spoke. I had to do something. I was sitting at the piano and deliberately dropped the hymnal on the piano. In that brief eye-lock moment, Linda knew she was in trouble. She poked at Martha and they both acted like nothing happened. As was typical of them.

Once a month on Sunday nights we had a potluck dinner. This family style buffet was in the church rectory and long tables with chairs on either side of the table was set up. Because we had grown accustomed to looking out for Martha and Linda's pranks, we sat the minister between them, her mother, Freida, on the other side of Martha and me on the other side of Linda, so "nothing would happen." Every church has members with oddities, or peculiarities, and our church was no exception. The very same woman the girls pranked almost every Tuesday night with their rendition of "Bringing in The Sheaves," sat on the other side of Freida. As was her custom, she would take her false teeth out, and set them above her plate next to her water glass. Spotting an opportunity, Martha dropped a napkin over those uppers and behind the minister's back handed them, unbeknownst to me, to Linda.

As Mrs. J began to fumble for her teeth she asked Martha, then Linda where her teeth were. A few snickers from all of us followed, but those teeth were gone! Where could they be? The girls were asked to empty out their purses and pockets, which they obediently did. If they did not have them, where could they be? We asked Mrs. J to look in her purse and a few of the younger congregants scurried along the floor in case the teeth had developed legs and walked off. Unable to find the missing teeth, we moved into the sanctuary for the evening service.

During the offering it was customary to bring the offering plates forward to be blessed. As the minister began his prayer, he thanked God for the multitude of blessings this small congregation was about to receive, "and yes Lord, please bring Mrs. J's teeth back to her!" As the offering plates were distributed and retrieved, he put his hand into his outer coat pocket, then turned to Martha and Linda and began to do a low he hee heeeee laugh! Low and behold those plates were brought forward for the Reverend to bless.

As he prayed, he slipped his hand back into his coat pocket and retrieved a napkin and put it in the offering plate. As he said his blessing, he gave thanks and praise that Mrs. J.'s teeth were delivered back to us. At that moment, everyone eyes opened and stared at the girls. But I knew who had put the teeth in the Reverend's jacket pocket. Come to think of it now, I do not believe Mrs. J ever took those teeth out again at the socials.

Calvary Baptist was such a blessing, and I counted my blessings as the kids remained in the fellowship of these friends, rather in places I would wonder and worry about.

Keeping kids busy with one thing or another is a good use of their abundant energy and vital to keeping them out of trouble. With one child you can hardly control them for long, and not even then. With nine you need a plan. The youth group, with so many young adults interested and engaged, thrived, and grew. And as my family grew up, they grew in their favor of the church, through their relationships and activities. The ultimate blessing was the remaining unity as we worshipped as a family.

Freida and I were a mainstay with the kids. For me though because of my music responsibilities at the church, and in my studio, it was mostly the Campus Life and outings. Some of their irreverent humor kept us all in stitches and maybe secretly we wished we had thought of that.

How Long Has It Been?

"Give thanks in all circumstances; for this is God's will for you in Christ Jesus."

I Thessalonians 5:18 (NIV)

Chapter 16

How Long Has It Been?

In early 1971 my husband's sister moved to San Diego after her husband died. Wanting to start over she asked to stay in the room we had taken Fred and Sam out of a few years earlier.

In-laws can suddenly become outlaws, in your mind, especially if you think they have overstayed their welcome. Even her easy laugh started to get on my nerves. Dutch has started going in the back yard to smoke a cigarette. That moved from the backyard to frequenting a bar in town. When I put my foot down about his drinking partner, she moved to an apartment in town. She frequently talked him into coming home later, and usually after drinking for a few hours. When she moved to Chula Vista, he started visiting her there, causing a huge riff to develop between all of us.

The more I fought this the more resentful I became. What was happening to my marriage? To the close relationship my husband and I had always had? Over the course of the next several months he went to church with me less and less until he stopped going altogether. Embittered, I blamed her for this. Deep within me, I knew he was at fault too, but blaming her was easier, because I was already mad enough at him! We stopped praying together but Dutch never stopped tithing or making sure I went to church. There was something about his tithing that was tied to his salvation.

Three of the kids were out of the house at the end of 1971. Sam was married, with the first grandchild due within weeks. Rod was gone to Westmont College in Santa Barbara. James was still in Colorado.

This time in my life was like no other before or since. The more I fought to maintain control, the less I had. You raise your kids to be independent adults, but they were still at home and practicing that skill every day with me. Linda's headstrong independence clashed with my need to keep her under my wing. The more we fought the more Dutch and I fought until mid-spring 1972. My way or the highway fighting with Linda abruptly ended when I told her to leave on her 18th birthday. At wits end I cried until I broke. In the moment that you give up, a peace comes over you. You are tired of the fight.

The thing is, the more you wrestle with your emotions, the more your emotions overtake your thoughts. I fought everything I could not control, which by this time was a lot. It was a total conundrum. The definition of **conundrum** is a situation where there is no clear right answer or no good solution. I felt like I was swinging at everything. How had my life come to this?

Wanting to run, but knowing better to stay put, was a daily struggle. These are natural feelings when you do not have a clear idea of what to do. I secretly prayed that Jesus would wave His hand over this situation and, like Matthew 8:23, calm the storm and the tumultuous waters. But I knew this would not happen.

Crying had not helped any more than fighting with my husband or the kids did. The fight was within me as I began to realize that wrestling with my emotions revealed more issues. Or was I wrestling with Spirit?

One late afternoon two women, Marlene and Christine, now a lifelong friend, knocked at my door. "You know my mother-in-law, Stella Tooker," said Christine. They both attended a church in National City. "We are looking for someone to replace our pianist, for our Gospel Group," said Christine. Marlene, who was their pianist, sat down and played my piano and said she loved it. I found myself saying, "Well, it's for sale!" "How much?" she asked. I sold it for $200 more than I paid, which was a 35% profit.

On July 3, they came and picked up the piano, leaving me just a few days to find another one. I called my go-to-piano-guy, Jeff. "You'll never believe this," he said, "but a couple, getting a divorce, just gave me their baby grand Yamaha to sell." "How much?" I excitedly said. "$2600," he said, matter-of-factly. "How much do you need?" I asked. "Oh, they need cash, right now," he said. I did not know how I was going to get a loan. In the 70's women, even if they were married, did not qualify for loans, even if they were on the title of a house with equity, let alone credit on their own.

 Mrs. Humphry, a piano student's mother, put in a good word at the bank and I got a loan, with a $65/month repayment.

When Marlene and Christine came back to get the piano they asked if I would play the piano for them. I had no idea it was an audition. They instantly loved my piano style and asked if I would consider playing for their group, The Calvaryheirs. Denny and Cherry, Avery, Christine Tooker, Glen and Betty Zucher, Tom James.

When I asked Dutch what he thought, he told me, "Do what you want. You're going to do it anyway." I went to the first rehearsal on Thursday night. Nothing like a healthy distraction to take your mind off your problems.

My piano studio was robust, and I taught over 40 students a week. That meant mornings were spent getting the house organized for the day, meals prepped for later so the afternoon and evening would accommodate a studio environment. Having fewer kids at home made it easier to keep the house quiet enough to conduct lessons.

James came home to tell us he had enlisted in the Army, stationed at Ft Lewis in Tacoma, Washington. We were left with the "lower fourth," Del, Dwayne Laurie and Walter at home.

Work was steady for Dutch and he steadily grew his business. He bought a panel van, a new pickup truck and equipment. It required he got a loan. Fireside thrift would not give a loan without my signature.

I would not sign the loan unless he got an insurance policy that paid at least half the loan, in case of an injury or something that caused him to be unable to work.

Dutch would frequently come home, after a long day, and ask me to make him a mustard pack. This consisted of one egg and 1 tablespoon of dried mustard, mixed into a paste, and put between two cloths pressed onto his back.

The combination made a heat that he said drew out the soreness in his lower back. After an extended period of this treatment, along with chiropractic adjustments, I worried something more was wrong. Now that is just like a woman to worry, right?

The chiropractor said he was in a hard line of work and maybe if he just eased up, it would make him feel better. Nothing like this ever happens to an entrepreneur. Whether you are running a piano studio or running a small business, you never take sick days. If the work is there you work - because you do not know when you will have work again. And there was plenty of time in the winter that he could not work.

The family doctor gave him pain pills or muscle relaxants. Whether it was the way my husband communicated with the doctor or the protocol of the day, I will never know why simple blood tests were not run. Just getting him to a doctor was a challenge.

I had been with the Calvaryheirs three months when Dutch said I needed to give notice I would be leaving the group. When he passed what looked like a pint of blood through his urine, he finally brought it to my attention. I immediately called a doctor. We were both scared.

It was a hot and humid August. The former family doctor had been replaced with a new and more accessible doctor in Coronado. After the examination the doctor immediately referred my husband to a urologist and team of specialists that ran several tests. The next day this new doctor confirmed our worst fears.

Dutch was diagnosed with kidney cancer, already metastasized. I could not even pronounce the word let alone wrap my mind around what this meant. In an instant my world changed.

Was this curable? Could I pray this out of him? Could God give me another miracle and cure this? As the doctor talked my mind went on overload. The only thing I recall with total clarity was that he said Dutch had 6 to 9 months to live. And to put his affairs in order.

Another wave of shock hit me as I watched the doctor and Dutch's eyes lock. How could this be? My kind and wonderful 53-year-old husband was all I could think of. Not him. Not now. Not us. No!

We had just celebrated our 24th wedding anniversary and often talked about what we would do when all the kids were grown. Traveling across the country, like we had when we first came to California, was what we often talked about. I choked back tears and put on a brave face, but I was totally shattered and scared for him.

While we worked against a looming deadline, Dutch asked if I thought it was a good idea for him to have the surgery. I held his hand and told him that this was one decision I could not make for him. This would have to be his decision but whatever he decided I said I would support him.

Within a week we miraculously were scheduled at the VA hospital in La Jolla for his surgery. Within three days he was immediately recommended for surgery to remove a kidney to relieve him of the terrible pain he was in.

If you have ever been in this situation, you know how painful this reality is. As the children were growing up, we had walked on ice before. We did not have insurance and somehow, we had made it through.

When you have a crisis there will be time for tears, but not when you are called on to be the strength and possibly only wage in the house. I had much to do to support Dutch's health crisis. Even if he could not work, my income needed to continue. As a music major at San Diego State University, Linda filled in as pianist, organist at the church, and as teacher for my students.

It takes a village, and usually starts with your own family. The head of our household was in the fight of his life. With cancer waging a war on his life, he fought hard to beat it. Surgery, chemo, miracle cancer drugs from Mexico, you name it he tried it. But nine months after that battle began, he lost it, just weeks after our 25th anniversary. And like the hero he was to me, he never backed down, whimpered or cried, "Why me?" His strength and endurance became mine.

His Eye is on the Sparrow

Therefore do not worry about tomorrow,
for tomorrow will worry about itself.
Each day has enough trouble of its own.

Matthew 6:34 (NIV)

182

Chapter 17

His Eye is on the Sparrow

"Just when you think it can't get worse, it can, and frequently does. So, this is a reminder to encourage you to stay in the mind of gratitude and prayer. This will help you see your situation much differently than if you give into your emotional state." These were words that stung me like a bee, said by the salesman I was talking to, when I was standing in a music store in downtown San Diego. But deep inside me, as much as I did not like what he said, there might be an element of truth I thought.

I was totally overwhelmed. With three minor children at home, facing a mountain of bills, I worried night and day. Looking around I thought about how I was going to pay for the house mortgage (we had paid his parents off in 1972 for the original down payment they loaned us), property insurance, car payments, food, utilities, new piano payments, outstanding doctor bills, and the business equipment.

When Dutch started his business in late 1972, we could never have known that three years later he would be in the fight for, and ultimately, lose his life. Whether or not you know how certain your life is going, or if you know where you want to go, there are still no guarantees.

He was so proud of starting that business. Since he had always worked for other companies, he had no equipment of his own and needed a loan to acquire it. After he acquired his business license, in early 1973 he went to Fireside Thrift to secure a business loan. The

183

equipment included one new 1-ton flatbed truck and one used panel van, the plaster gun, 2 mixers, scaffolding, generator, compressors – in all about $20,000 of equipment.

Fireside required my husband to use the equity of the house as a guarantee of repayment. When Dutch asked me to co-sign for the loan I learned of the terms and refused to sign without an insurance policy guaranteeing at least $10,000 repayment against the debt, in the unlikely event he got sick or injured. We would have purchased the amount of insurance for the entire amount, but it was expensive, and we never thought we would need it. I did not know anything about debt or insurance, but I did know enough that equity had value and debt could take it away. That was God's hand on my shoulder. If I had not insisted on the insurance, I would have had to repay the almost $17,000 remaining on the loan at the time of my husband's death. We thought the business was the best bet he had taken because 1974 was his best year ever, and we were elated his risk appeared to be paying off.

Without a second income in the house where was I going to get the funds to pay the debt, cost of living, and stay in the house?

I immediately started to sell the equipment so I could pay off the remaining Fireside Thrift debt that was not covered by the insurance. Both trucks were immediately sold. The material yard let me sell the concrete gun on their property, where it was sold to pay the outstanding material balance.

It had not occurred to me that someone would want to deceive or take advantage of a grieving widow. When you are at your lowest emotionally take guard because that is when you are at your weakest and most vulnerable. I received an invoice from an attorney in La Jolla. It was a staggering bill and I called the attorney to ask why I was receiving an inheritance tax bill. Without hesitation he said, "You just inherited your husband's half of the property, so you have to pay an inheritance tax." I explained I did not owe it and he insisted I did.

When you are in a vulnerable state do not be stoic, like I was. Ask for help. Ask your friends if they know someone that knows something about this or that if you are not certain about what you are hearing or seeing. Do not assume everyone has your best interest at heart, or that you must carry the burden. That is one lesson I know is vital to tell you as the reader. Even though I successfully negotiated a smaller debt, I unnecessarily paid that bill, when I desperately needed that money to pay off other bills. *That mistake was a scam.* California is a community property state and also the way we held title. I was entitled to take the other half when my husband died, without owing an inheritance tax.

When Dutch got his diagnosis, we decided to close the business down. Despite closing this in August 1974, I still received an income tax bill to pay our projected quarterly income tax. Without work how could we pay it? Or if we would not be receiving any more income, why would we even have to pay it? The blessings of our good friends at the Nestor Methodist Church took up a love offering for us. When we received the proceeds, miracle of all miracles was that it was one dollar less than the amount we owed for taxes.

Each night as I lay in my bed, I remembered these blessings and miracles. But soon I would forget them as I woke to reach for my husband's hand that used to be there, to comfort me, and reassure me that everything would be ok, and we would somehow get through this. As I fought back the bitter tears, I swallowed the reality of each and every day, and knew I would have to figure this out and brave it without him. "Lord, how am I going to get through this?"

As I lay in the bed weeping, thinking, praying, pleading with my thoughts and conversations with God, they intertwined so that my thoughts and words began to be conversations with God. I said, "I lost my best friend and partner, God." God assured me I was not the only person had who experienced this loss. "Many others have suffered the same. This may be an opportunity to share how you get through this," I heard God whisper. Yes, other grieving widows, widowers, and even business owners who lost their partners, have a lot to figure out and a lot of grieving to go through, I thought. *The only way out is through*, became my mantra, as I repeatedly said it when I was scared.

Was I losing my mind? It sounded absurd. But I had learned not to question God. As I continued to talk with God I wondered and asked, "What's the lesson? What am I supposed to learn from this? And hurry up God! I need to find this out as soon as possible."

My husband was only 53 when he died. I was 44, a widow with four minor children to raise, and a lot of bills. How was I going to do this, and make enough income that the two of us made before? I was so exhausted from these thoughts and crying that I would fall asleep, only to awake a few hours later, and start this cycle again. Eventually dawn would come, and I would force myself to get up, get in the shower, and have one last cry before starting the day to figure this out.

My youngest son, Wally, who was only 9 at the time of his Dad's death, came to me one morning and said, "Don't cry Mom, I'll help." When the innocent thoughts of another human being remind you of your responsibility, you naturally come back to it, and change your attitude in prayer. That new attitude will lead you to the point of gratitude and eventually latitude of your situation. You stop feeling sorry for yourself and start figuring things out. Each step is another step towards your recovery. Keep taking those steps, do not stop, and suddenly, in retrospect, you will see how far you have come.

I was dealing with other issues with the children still at home. Dwayne, Laurie, and Walter were my biggest concerns. Dwayne's risky behavior got him in fights and Laurie had retreated into her own thoughts. Wally was comic relief who always seemed contented. We were all dealing with out grief differently.

When one of my older sons had started teenage drinking, my husband and I sent him off to my brother's. When the next son was under the influence of alcohol, I was forced to deal with the situation head on. But I was not prepared as a single parent to deal with this on my own. I was struggling with how to make ends meet, deal with my own grief, and confront my own issues that I had with my husband's drinking before he got sick.

When Dwayne got into trouble, I was grateful for the help I got. Linda stepped up and leaned in. Dwayne got the attention an only child would get, and he craved, when he moved in with Linda. She was teaching and within several months would embark on a music tour with a band, leaving San Diego behind. One of the guys' Linda was dating before she left moved into Linda's condo, maintaining stability until Dwayne moved on. He moved into his own apartment, with another friend, and finished high school, which seemed miraculous by the eroded standards of my family's embrace of education.

My nightly thoughts subtly shifted from despair and grief. In the early hours of the morning, after some tossing and turning, I realized my mind had shifted to, "It's worth the wait." Curious at this thought I got up and opened my Bible to **Psalms 27:14**, "Wait on the LORD: be of good courage, and He shall strengthen thine heart: wait, I say, on the LORD." This mantra became my new attitude and gave me renewed hope.

I had not figured anything out yet, but you cannot hear the sound of the Angels, see the light of the dawn, or walk in faith when you hold onto despair. Was that the lesson? I was so caught up with "Poor me," that most of my time had been spent at my own pity party. No company was needed to thoroughly enjoy my own misery. I knew better than to talk to anyone. They might look at my situation and wonder what I was going on about. Sometimes our situation looks completely normal to the outside. And sometimes our situation actually is normal, but we fail to see it.

What was I learning? That emotions lie to you. They say your circumstance is far worse than anyone else's – how else can you stay in your pity party if your situation were suddenly improved by looking at it differently?

We all have worry. It is a human condition. But the farther we get from God and His Perfection, the more we find and get to worry about.

In Dr. Jeremiah's Study Bible, he lays out in his interpretation of Matthew 6:25-31, God's 5 reasons we should not or do not need to worry. For your reference, it is worth noting.

25. Worry is inconsistent. If we trust God to provide us with life, why would we not trust Him with our daily needs.

26. Worry is irrational. If God cares for the birds, who do not seem to have a worry about what to eat, can God also care for us? Are we not more valuable than a bird?

27. Worry is ineffective. Can you add one cubit (the length from an average elbow to the tip of the middle finger) to our importance or life by worrying?

28. Worry is illogical. If God can clothe the lilies of the field, can He not also clothe us?

31-32 Worry is not a part of God's plan. We act just like those that who do not have any faith or belief in God when we worry.

My pastor, Dr Jeremiah, goes on to teach that we need a system of priorities, "Seek first the kingdom of God and His righteousness," (Matthew 6:33), and, a strategic plan, "Do not worry about tomorrow, for tomorrow will worry about its own things," (Matthew 6:34).

Each day had its own challenges. I had growing strength in my resolve and responsibility to myself and my children. But it was a daily walk. One day at a time.

After selling as much of my husband's equipment as possible, I looked seriously at my real estate business, but knew it was not steady money. I needed a job that had steady and dependable income and started looking. I was teaching as many hours as were available for my students, but that did not cover the amount needed.

I even went to the police department to apply for a job, and was told, "You're too old. We don't hire people your age!" the officer told me. "Well how old do you think I am?" I asked. "Late 30s," he said. This was long before equal opportunity and other employment protection and discrimination laws.

Although I am not sure he thought I was asking to work as a law enforcement officer, but I was looking for clerical work. Feeling deflated, at least I did not look my age, I thought. The job I had taken as organist at the Methodist church, when Linda was no longer able to maintain it in her schedule, was not enough to cover the gap of my new financial responsibilities.

This spurred me on to figure out how to creatively close the gap. I went to the South Bay School District and asked to speak to the music department chair for the district, who was Mary Ellen Woodhouse at the time. After filling out my application she came out and asked me to come to her office. "Where have you been?" she asked. Somewhat dumbfounded, I asked, "What do you mean?" "We have been looking for you. We called your house several times. We needed you yesterday." She asked me to sit down and play a few songs and asked how I would teach them to the students. Her last question was, "When can you start?"

By now you should be thinking, "Yup, another miracle," but I had another thought. Why did I worry. Why did I not trust God more? Clearly the answer had arrived, while I was in the middle of despair and anxiety but was so busy with pity that I could not or would not pay attention.

It is also important to point out that even in my own then-church, there was not a lot of encouragement or support. Maybe congregants view an employee of the church differently, or maybe they do not see us as having needs too.

Now I do not mean I needed a cheerleading squad to rah-rah me into the end zone, high-five me that I made it through another week, or take a love offering to help me meet my monthly shortfalls.

What I mean, is that I needed spiritual encouragement. I am reminded of it every time I turn on the television and hear about another tragedy. Whether it was Sandy Hook Elementary, San Bernardino, Navy Yard, Baptist church or a Synagogue's mass shootings, civil disturbances that end in violence, or a super fire that wipes out the only road in or out.... There is no shortage of the need for prayer. But when I hear, "Our prayers are with you," I think, "Why not pick up the phone or, if possible, pay a visit and actually pray with that person?" Need is immediate. The human touch is a gift of God and giving it can bring the presence of the Lord and immediate relief.

I am grateful for my support. From my family to the church, to my friends and all who gave their time and support. This got me through some tough times.

When you do not know what you need, it is also ok just to say," Pray with me. Hold my hand and tell me it is going to be ok." For some, this is enough. For others you may need to rinse and repeat this process.

And if you are the care giver, instead of saying, "I'll pray for you" or "I know how you feel" or start telling them about yourself, remember it is not about you in that moment. But is about *what you do* in that moment. Ask if you can pray right then and there. Even if you do not know what to say, your sincerity in that moment will show your compassion and empathy. Then pay it forward, because you never know where the help is needed most, or who needs it most. God is certainly watching over us. We can come out of despair as much as we can lift, with our words, and deeds to help each other.

As more of my time was available now, my ministry in music with the Calvaryheirs picked up momentum. The song I wrote, "Thank You Jesus," two weeks before my husband died, was now being recorded, as we prepared to go into the recording studio and cut our first album.

We had talked about going into the studio many times because we had a great repertoire of songs ready. But we never had the money. That is, until another miracle. My good friend and member of the group, Christine Tooker, also the daughter in law of my very good friend, Stella Tooker, who passed away a few months earlier, came to the group with an announcement. "My mother-in-law left $2,000 in her will to seed the money needed to record."

"Thank you, Jesus, for the peace you have given me today.

Your great love and wonderous grace brought me through my fears."

How Am I Supposed To Let Go

Be strong and bold; have no fear or dread of them, because it is the Lord your God who goes with you; he will not fail you or forsake you.

DEUTERONOMY 31:6 (NSRV)

Chapter 18

How Am I Supposed to Let Go?

After the darkest winter of my life, I began to see the hope of spring as my life without my husband began to stabilize. Dutch had been sick for nine months, and I was consumed with his health and well-being. But after he passed, I was now consumed with my own financial survival.

Within a few months I was working 13 different elementary schools in the school district (K-6). The new job gave me confidence because I knew what I was doing, plus it also improved my self-esteem. Each school appreciated me more than the other, and I looked forward to my daily tasks, and how I would impart music to the public. Teaching songs and rhythm, I watched the kids' eyes light up when I walked in, and the teacher's appreciative eyes that there was another diversion to focus these kids' energy on. I started at 6:30 am, then raced home to teach my first piano student at 3pm until 6 or 7pm. Once a week there was still the choir rehearsal at the church and of course Sunday services.

After a few years I wanted more meaning and purpose to the education I was delivering. I was starting to feel the pressure of overwhelm again. What was causing that? I should be grateful that I had all this work, and I was, so what was I feeling anxious about?

Call it divine discontentment. When you are dissatisfied with the status quo, start listening within. Quiet your mind and your thoughts, which can be exceedingly difficult with so many messages, thoughts, and distractions. Some people meditate.

Take time to hear the still small voice within you. That is God speaking to you. Sometimes God has to send multiple messages because we do not listen. We think a timely call, a comment made that has a message only you understand is a coincidence. Even the discovery of something you cannot explain, you easily slough off the explanation as a mere chance. And sometimes the message gets delivered on a billboard because you are too hard-headed to get the consistent messages, as it did earlier in my life.

But at this point, I had learned to value the quiet morning time and my devotional. It always included reading scripture and spending time in prayer and listening.

As I had often done, I would ask God to guide me about my discontentment and what else He had in store for me. This prayer was fulfilled shortly. One day, a South Bay Christian School director called and asked if I would be interested in teaching high school. Although the pay was less, so were the hours. However, I did not need as much money as I needed when my husband passed away, because I learned to manage my money. It is amazing what you can learn to do when you must. I paid off the Fireside Thrift loan, piano, organ and only needed to fund the house payments, insurance, taxes, and other necessities. I never thought I would be in the position to fulfill the financial obligations I had previously relied on my husband for. God is good.

But my needs were met. I had everything I needed. Maybe not everything I wanted, but I had what I needed. I stopped worrying about turning on the heat in the winter and started enjoying the fireplace my husband had had built for me in 1974, when his business was good. I had the money to burn cords of wood. If I had not been so busy trying to sort out that living thing – paying bills, mothering the children still at home, and keeping up with my jobs, I could have written a cookbook on the 1001 ways to fix hamburger when the kids were growing up. But as each week passed, and then months, we could occasionally eat out. Surely goodness and mercy shall follow me to the end of my life.

This extra time let me begin to think about socializing again. That had been completely put out of my mind as I busied and hurried and worried and prayed. But this slow down let me begin to appreciate time. Time is the true paradox. We have as much as there is and yet we never have enough of it. Slowing down allowed me time to enjoy the kids a little more and help them.

Sunday afternoons we frequently stopped at a Mission Bay hotel, the Atlantis, for brunch. Before Dwayne moved in with Linda he would often opt to just go home after church and not join Laurie, Wally and me. Sometimes we would go to Pacific Ocean Park, sometimes the zoo, or even movies. Over a short period of time, Laurie had started becoming more independent too.

Wally wanted to learn how to shoot a BB gun and the older kids were not around. This made me reach out to the new Big Brothers organization. They sent out a retired Navy SEAL. Come to think of it I do not believe he ever showed Wally how to shoot either, but the one night a week they spent, I was grateful Wally had a strong male figure who took an interest in him. He taught Wally how to swim in the ocean and took him to some baseball games.

Laurie was more social but did not want the one-on-one of a Big Sister. She frequented one of the neighbor's kids house and decided to play match maker with her friend's father.

This became the beginning of a wonderful friendship that has endured to this day. While we had a lot in common, I was not interested in the kind of help he offered. He was more paternal to me and I really wanted more than a problem solver. I cannot exactly say what I wanted, but I did enjoy the attention and the pleasantness that the relationship had. At 46, I also wondered if I would even have another opportunity to meet someone special or if I should respond to the ardent attempts of my suitor. One day, however, I overheard him talking with someone that he was not sure if it would be me or another person he named.

That was it. Despite all my worries that this may be the last chance to remarry, I put those thoughts aside and ended the relationship cordially.

As I busied myself with a new set of students, adults who wanted to learn how to play piano, wanted these lessons only in the mornings. Since I only taught school twice a week, I had a few mornings available.

Teaching adults was rewarding. Every lesson included a little friendship, adult conversation, and sometimes a little therapy. I am not sure who benefited more, my students or me.

One of those students was taking lessons because her father had just bought her a piano. After a second or third lesson she said, "You've got to meet my dad! You're just like him!" I thought to myself, "Would I want anyone like me?" but I was curious enough to want to meet him.

I went with Kathy to a city council meeting, where I met her dad, Felix Hanley. He was well dressed and well spoken. But he was older, and I thought maybe a little too old for me. A few nights later he invited me to join him and his family for dinner. His daughter, and her husband and two kids, gave a verbal resume of his past twenty-five years. He proudly watched them recant his history with the railroad in Baltimore, MD. He represented the railroad's union as a liaison and representative to Washington, DC, the last four years of his service, and there were a lot of entertaining stories about meeting this or that dignitary or politician. He was not particularly impressed with titles and opted to take retirement and moved to San Diego to be closer to his only daughter.

His family repeatedly invited us over until we became comfortable on our own. I admired his intelligence and sincerity. He lost no time in letting me know that he wanted to help me raise the rest of the family.

I had been a widow for three years by then, but when he bought a ring and presented it, I realized my heart remained with my husband still, and I refused it. I was so shocked at the thought of committing to another person, I cut off the relationship. *Till death do us part* were vows I took seriously. How was I supposed to let go?

Over the course of the next several weeks I went on with my business, without giving this decision a second thought. But as I sat in the quietness of a particular morning devotional, my thoughts suddenly turned to those vows. In fact, it was death that did make my husband and I part. Did I need to wait until I was dead too to understand that I had already fulfilled those vows? God seemed to be pulling at those thoughts and gently reminded me that my prayers were being answered. I asked, "Well, what did I ask for?" "For your loneliness to be replaced. For someone to help you with the challenges you are facing with the second wave of teenagers…" At the mere thought of the word teenagers, I literally snapped out of my quiet time and thought, "Oh boy, what did I do?" as I picked up the phone and called Felix. Was he surprised to hear from me! It was early October and I told him, "If you are still interested in being a part of my family, make it December 15, when school is closed for the winter break, and I have more time. We'll do this at my church."

I am not sure if it was the commando-style orders I gave him that prompted his next course of action, or that he knew he had better take my change of heart seriously, but on December 15, 1978, I married my second husband.

Blending two families can be very tricky. I did not think I had many issues to face with my kids' acceptance of my new husband, and stepfather, because most of them were already grown and gone.

Fred and Vickie and their children, Jennifer, Matthew and Courtney lived in San Jose. James, now divorced, had one daughter, Heather, and had moved from Washington to San Jose. Fred, James, and Del had joined the union and worked the San Jose plaster trade.

Sam and Julie were in Garden Grove with their two children, Jason and Shawna.

None of them had seemed to be as interested in what I was doing, at least until I announced I was getting married again.

Rod, who lived in Santa Barbara since he had moved there after high school graduation, and Linda, who had just returned from a tour in Japan, were stand offish to "Han", his nickname from day 1. It would not take long to hear from all the kids who no longer lived at home, how different he was. They seemed to be more concerned that Han would take over my life that I had just reestablished for myself. Nothing could be farther from the truth. At some point you have to make decisions for yourself that others are simply not going to like. That is harder to do as you get older. More than you can imagine.

The kids were right. Han was different. He followed me in what I was doing with the Calvaryheirs, even carrying equipment. He made me feel like I was taken care of, that he had my back. He advised me on financial matters, on repairs that needed to be done at a house he did not even live in yet, and the problems I had with the two kids I had at home, Laurie and Wally, each with their own challenges.

You may have a child or "know of someone else's" that will challenge your parental authority until it is worn down or worn out. It can make you feel like you are being tested beyond your endurance. Your underage child is still your responsibility though, and you are legally and spiritually accountable for them. If you do not stand your ground, though, you will regret it and, in the end, their consequences remain with them the rest of their adult lives.

It is still hard to believe that Felix still said "I do" given the exacerbating circumstances that would continue to unfold until all my children left home. His family was grown, with his oldest son in Australia, a second son, in Baltimore and a daughter, Kathy and son, Michael, here in San Diego.

But we had the shared loss of a spouse in common. By contrast, his children were, initially, delighted their father had found someone he cared for after being a widower for the past 12 or 15 years.

Felix put order and rules and structure where I had become too tired to enforce. He held the kids accountable for going to school, when they would have preferred the zoo, goofing off, or hanging out with friends, to the structure and responsibility of classes. He made me become more responsible too. I stopped giving into the arguments that had previously broken me down.

Han stood behind me and supported this very tough walk-the-line decision and I was fortunate to have his support.

Parents make tough decisions along the way. Frequently we ask ourselves, "Could I have done better?" or "Did I do the right thing?" and sometimes we must rely on our moral compass and walk with God for our reassurance. The worst thing you can do as a parent is vacillate. What I mean is make your decision, then walk it back, then regret the walk back and have a firmer resolve; then regret it and walk it back again. Make a decision, then make the decision right. Time heals all wounds. And they have. It took decades. But I do not regret taking a stand for what I believe in and especially for instilling my values in my children. Proverbs 22:6 says, "Train a child in the way he should go, and when they are older, they will not leave it."

Wally was going to Christian school, where I was teaching, but he had started walking off the campus and going home. Felix took to writing Senator Cranston about the new trade school, Job Corp, that had just leased space at Ream Field. They offered an 18- month program that would also deliver a GED and a trade. It was not free. I do not know when he had time to apply for it, but Felix told me the *scholarship* had been received. This came at a time that Wally needed more structure than he would accept from us under his new circumstances.

There was a clear need for the male leadership that Felix provided, and I was grateful that I did not face the numerous challenges alone, that would be on the horizon.

He Is Faithful To The End

Because of the Lord's great love we are
not consumed,
for his compassions never fail.
They are new every morning;
great is your faithfulness.

Lamentations 3:22-23 (KJV)

Chapter 19

He is Faithful to the End

A second marriage comes with a lot of challenges that I could not begin to fully comprehend, until after I got over the need to please my children. This did not happen until I married Han. Dating life for a second marriage should be short. Especially if you bring 25 years of a prior marriage's experience with you. It is either going to work or not. You already know what marriage is about, and there should be no surprise expectations. Since Han had made it through the dating stage, where every date was at the church or a church-related event, we figured out how to hold hands, acknowledge a smile that meant we knew what our opinion on a matter was or not, and what made each other laugh. We figured this would make us want to celebrate more of life's moments shared together.

Despite this, our first year wasn't a cakewalk. We were grown adults. I was in my late forties, just getting my second wind. With seven children grown or having left home already, I still had two underage children to raise. Had, had been retired for a few years, and his four children were grown, living their own lives.

For starters, you are not a beginner. You may be starting over, but not from scratch. For instance, you are not concerned about starting a family, because you each already have one. However, even if the attraction is novel, you still have to work out your couple's code, how you communicate, how you function as a couple, without kids, as if you never had any, then figure out how to be a couple on your own with what is left of each other's lives together.

Then blend. Ha! That is the tough part. This is what you have an advocate for. Going to God in prayer was something I had learned to lean in on with my first husband. I had discovered that my second husband's relationship with his first wife did not establish prayer habits as their foundation. A devout Catholic relationship has many rituals to depend on, to get a relationship through the course of life, but daily prayer was not one of them.

A walk with Christ is not about rituals. You are not working for the *establishment or maintenance* of the Catholic church anymore; you are working with and for Christ. Han let people know this was new to him. To anyone that listened. And he was a good student. He let me know, when he heard a sermon, if the speaker was a "crackpot" or an inspiration. And our walk in life became different by the end of the first year. Love the one you are with throughout life, to the end of time, and that is with Christ.

His children had very distinctive lives he had helped shape. I needed some help for just the remaining two and he stood up to the task. He never tried to be "daddy" to my children. That can be a disaster, even if the real daddy is not in the picture, unless the children have no other point of reference.

He was already a father to his own grown children, but this would be a monumental task for anyone reading this and contemplating a second marriage that has children, especially with a woman that had nine children that were not his! A smaller man would not have contemplated or embraced the notion that the "pay" was low, but the company was worth it! But he did. And that says a lot about him. He may have questioned this over in his mind, but he never once said it out loud. He wrote Wally a note once that said, "I don't want to be your dad or a father to you. I just want to be a mentor." Wally and Han got along well. 1 out of 9 odds are not something anyone would want to bet on. Most of the kids had already spent 20+ years of their lives with their own father and were mourning his loss. They did not resent Han, but they kept their distance.

On the other hand, I had been able to maneuver my new position, as his wife, and become a friend to his children, even to this day.

But he was outnumbered with my nine. Despite this, he did not make enemies and managed to set boundaries diplomatically. That was something I could not do. I either feared if I did, I would lose the relationship with my children, and balanced it with his lack of fear if I did.

Many people make the mistake that your adult children somehow want to be introduced to your mate's adult children. You still have the individual work of being a single parent to your children's lives, but do not make the mistake that blending the two imperfect families will perfect something, even if it's only in your mind, unless they are very young and underage.

We soon discovered having annual passes to the San Diego Zoo was the perfect distraction to everything and went as often as we could., sometimes two or three times a week. Movies, theatre and, of course, my performances with the Calvaryheirs were things we enjoyed doing together.

After Laurie left, we went into couples' therapy. We were both headstrong and neither wanted to compromise, something that is needed to make a relationship work. Compromise is a lot harder in a second marriage, and particularly if you have both become independent of needing anyone's opinion besides yours.

We also took frequent trips to Arizona, where my mother had relocated, after selling the farm in North Dakota. The harsh winters were behind her as she opted for the high desert. The desert was no match for her green thumb. Her double wide soon had plenty of color from the numerous bougainvillea vines, even managing a small garden into her 80s.

We started to receive his family as guests. After a few visits I realized they were just as concerned about their dad and his decision to marry me, as many of my own had voiced their opinions early on. There were just a lot more opinions and children of my own, that even if his children had objected, it had not amounted to much, or he just did not tell me. This may have played on his mind and even given him pause for thought, as would be natural. But the biggest help was that the matchmaker, his daughter, lived in town and she frequently told him how lucky he was to have me. Although I agree with Kathy, you cannot get a better cheerleader than that!

As my routines became more, well, routine, the kids stopped raiding the refrigerator and leaving without so much as stopping to visit. They previously visited, but now said they felt more reserved with my new husband there. They said they just needed to stop and check on me – not visit. They just grabbed and ran. Eventually that stopped. I learned that if you carry enough things in the refrigerator they do not like, or they think it is something new, or ewwww! they will not try it. Life settled into a routine.

By then, Fred and Sam had moved back to San Diego and remained in the plaster trade. Rod was married and had started his own family. Even Linda had gotten married.

After a few years of marriage, I stopped working at the Christian High School because I was tired of teaching. That is when we started taking more day trips. I still maintained my piano students and work at the church and started to paint more frequently.

Before we got married, I had started taking oil painting lessons in 1976 to fill a void after my first husband passed away. Since I had grown up with my mom's voice still in my head, "Idle hands are a workshop for the devil" I kept my mind off my grief and got my hands busy painting. Han encouraged me to continue taking classes to improve my skills. This turned out to be a great decision and offered additional income when I least expected it. I also won awards.

Painting gave me a sense of freedom. I had no idea this latent talent was even there. Being able to take what I envisioned, recalled, or imagined in my thoughts, and transfer those images to canvas was deeply satisfying. Painting the sky became a new experience. Who knew there were so many colors in the sky? When I went to New Mexico the skies contained purple. Desert and oceans became my passion to paint. Everywhere I went painted a new image in my mind, and a race began to recreate it on canvas. Commissioned paintings only inspired me to paint more because it was evidence that what I really enjoyed was productive and profitable.

In 1981, Wally graduated from the Job Corp and met a friend named Gino, whose dad was a developer. They hit it off. So much that Wally and Gino got their own version of a Shangri-La apartment. They were so proud of their place. One day, Wally came over with a cute little Chow puppy someone gave him. He had not thought dog ownership through, since he was not able to keep the puppy in the apartment all day while he worked, and could not take him to work. He came over *to just show and tell* Han the dog. I have to say it was love at first sight. After Wally explained his personal dilemma, Han offered Wally $25 and generous visitation rights for the pup. After a small exchange, the pup became ours and that love affair evolved. This was Wally's idea of perfect dog ownership. I cannot say we were disappointed. The dog filled Han's idle time when I was busy, as he trained the dog. Then a bird arrived, then a cat. He was an animal lover and had a lot of love in his heart to give. Animals are so wonderful – they give everything without judgement or reserve unconditionally. Truly God's gift to man.

I was still in school. The school of humility. Learning to blend your will with someone who is equally as strong without you, requires a lot of giving in. A Christian walk of faith cannot be done without being humble though. Thy will, not my will, be done. Without humility you may not be able to do God's will.

Let us just say you feel really convicted by God in your daily devotion or prayer to do something, but then decide, "I'm not gonna do that," and eventually make a believable excuse to yourself not to. That' is pride getting in the way. And that pride can lead to you making mistakes. There is no second- guessing God… Han was brought into my life for a reason. How could I say, "Do it only my way," and have that man believe I was directed by God every single time I used this excuse to commandeer him to do it my way. And how would I justify this in the eyes of God as righteous?

I have said it before, blending a family, especially two people as independent as Han and I were separately, is difficult, at best. So, if you are lucky, paying attention to humility may prevent you from eating a lot of crow.

We had been married a few years when my Aunt Alice, my dad's younger sister, had gotten up in years and was no longer able to drive. She and my Uncle Herb never had children and nieces and nephews often picked up the responsibility children might have. More of her thoughts and time were consumed about her last years here on earth. So, we visited often.

When my Dutch and I initially came to California it was Aunt Alice's older sister, Kate who hosted him while I stayed back in Redlands, waiting for him to establish his business and bring the family to San Diego. Alice was a retired schoolteacher who had come to San Diego, after relocating with her husband, Herb Good, from Visalia in the late 1960s. They bought a house near Southwestern College and we visited them often. He loved coming to our house for holiday meals and enjoyed having my boys around. Aunt Alice did not share his enthusiasm. Maybe she had had enough children at school. I remember he asked the boys to work clearing some brush on their property. Aunt

Alice wanted to deduct the cost of the boys' lunch from their wages, but Uncle Herb said, "No, that wouldn't be right."

They had only been in their new house about four years when Uncle Herb suddenly had a massive heart attack and died. He was a good and generous man who had doted on his wife. Since they never had children my cousins, Roberta, Doug and I felt responsible for my aunt. When Doug moved to Northern California the responsibility fell on Roberta and me. After Uncle Herb died though, Aunt Alice became a more frequent guest at our holiday dinners. She had a little money tucked away and frequently went on cruises. My son, Rod, would ask her directly, "Aunt Alice, why does your skin look so taut and red every time you go on a "cruise"?" as he used his two hands to put air quotes around the word "cruise". Come to think of it, she did look like she was getting a little cosmetic surgery after she returned from a few of these trips, I thought. But I would quickly shoo Rod's comments under the table and just laugh, "Ha, ha! Kids! They say the darndest things!" But she sat across from Rod and would just eye him and raise one eyebrow – something that nearly every family member understands the meaning of. Rod could be taunting. Aunt Alice had developed tremors and you guessed it, Rod picked right up on that and would mimic her when he thought she was not watching.

Ok, so maybe I had a little guilt.

After visiting her one day I was getting ready to leave her house. She had seemed very agitated as I was getting ready to leave. Leaping up she said, "Don't leave yet!" as she shook some papers in her right hand. Continuing, she said, "I need you to take me to the Greenwood Cemetery. I want you to see something right now." I said I needed to get home. The more I explained, the more agitated and relentless she became, but she would not tell me what she wanted me to see, as she shook those papers.

I had a sudden flashback of how Aunt Alice was reminiscent of my grandmother, Mora Harchanko, her mother. Mora would pray her morning chant that quickly became a howl followed by wailing, as she rocked into a trance until she was done. That could go on for a while - Or ten minutes when my mother would knock on her door to stop her. By the time my mom did something the whole house was spooked and agitated because we had been instructed to maintain radio silence while Mora "prayed." And honestly, who could think of eating breakfast while this was going on?

I was afraid Aunt Alice had the potential to go on longer. Without wanting to stir this memory any further, I quickly picked up the phone and called Han to tell him I would be late. As I ushered her into the car, she was tight lipped and would not say what she wanted to show me. She would only say, "Wait till we get there." Oh, you bet, I am going to wait. What in the world could be so important that she would be so agitated and yet insistent that I share her secret that can only be seen at a cemetery?!

When we got there, she directed me to a newly erected mausoleum, called the "Court of Wisdom" and walked in and pointed to one of the drawers with no name and said, "This is where I am going to be buried." Then she pointed to the spot next to hers and said she bought that one too, as she shook the paper which was evidently a receipt for her purchase. Puzzled, I asked, "Who is that one for?" knowing that my uncle was dead and buried years earlier, and she had no children. "Well I'm going to have Herb exhumed, of course, and have him put there immediately." "Of course," I thought, as I rolled my eyes. "Who else would join you in the Court of Wisdom?" She suddenly turned on her heel and walked straight to the "clubhouse", where a jolly undertaker greeted us and walked us into a room full of caskets. I thought I was going to pass out. I had seen death, but never the preparation for it. She pointed out the one she had selected and cheerfully said she had upgraded it to include an innerspring mattress. *Really?*

Oh boy, I could not wait to get out of there. It gave me the willies and I could not wait to deliver her back home. "You've been alone too long," I thought.

Later I told Han about this. Even though we concluded she could stay with us, I was bothered that she was making all these preparations, but not with her permanent landlord, our Heavenly Father. She avoided all conversations about that. Uncle Herb was a 32nd degree Mason and that was her religion. No wonder she was worried, I thought.

In early 1979 I mentioned to her I would be visiting my sister, Edna, in New Mexico. Aunt Alice volunteered that I could drive her new Oldsmobile, so she could go along. Han had no desire to see my sister, Edna, and her husband. Wally was game for anything and went along. However, there was no driving her car, as she controlled who was driving and drove all the way there and back, until she was stopped by a state trooper for going 90 MPH. When she was asked if she knew how fast she was going, she replied, "No officer. I'm just a little old lady." He wrote her a ticket anyway and she fumed but drove all the way back, saying nothing. Prior to being stopped though, she kept saying, "I have to change my living quarters, I can't keep living alone." When I asked if she could live with one of her sisters, Aunt Lillian or Aunt Kate, or a favored niece Roberta or nephew Douglas, she said, "No. No one can take care of me." So, I offered to let her live with us.

In 1981, as her mental capacity diminished, she sold her house and moved in with Han and me. She lived here two and a half years. Even though she went to the store with me she never seemingly bought anything. Despite this, we found a closet full of 'empties' after she moved out. Vodka was her preferred drink. How she got this delivered or when is beyond my comprehension since I was always with her. Maybe a visitor brought them. But quarts? And I always thought she was a *teetotaler*. Her refusal to speak about God always ended with, "Don't talk to me about God. You are scaring the hell out of me." When Aunt Alice started wandering off, we started putting locks on the doors she could not reach. She never forgot that she was a teacher and people respected her and she let us know that. But when asked what year it was, she did not know. Han showed great compassion and care for her and felt protective toward her. We moved her to assisted living where she lived out her years. And you bet, she now resides in the Hall of Wisdom on her inner spring mattress, and I'm sure Herb rests better for that.

Aunt Alice was a good diversion in our marriage. It gave us a common goal to take care of her, but it did take a lot of effort and could be challenging. There was some comic relief because under the circumstances that could be trying, and you just had to laugh. Maybe Rod had it right after all.

In early 1985 I found out my mother was sick and had just had surgery in Prescott, AZ, near her home. She had suffered for years with diverticulitis, but she would never discuss the details or extent of her pain or self-remedies with her doctor. She came from a different era that you did not share something so personal as to discuss your own health. She had a freezer and cabinet full of all sorts of remedies and probably suffered for many years. When she was diagnosed with diverticulitis we were caught by surprise. My sister-in-law, Betty, my brother Ted's wife, came with Linda and me to care for Mom after her surgery. It hurt me to see my mother so frail and unable to care for herself. A woman who had seen many trials and tribulations and had never complained was suddenly dependent on the love and care of her immediate family. It was a humbling experience. Her faith was great though. It was solid as a rock. If this was her time to go, she was ready.

After a few days I insisted that she come to San Diego where I would be able to care for her. Betty, who was already there, helped my mother ready herself for her trip to California and her final move.

My mother enjoyed the living room couch because it was in the middle of the action and in the central part of the house. The piano studio, now located where the garage had been turned into a den, always seemed too far away for her liking. Han would sit with her in the afternoons while I taught piano and she would fall asleep listening to the sounds of the household. She enjoyed being able to be with us, but she was very weak. My aunts who were still alive, Aunt Lillian and Aunt Kate, visited. Mom liked the quiet, but she liked it better when I would play for her. She would request old Russian hymns I had grown up on. But she knew her time was limited. Your loved ones know this before you do. And it is important that you actually listen to their dying wishes. They do not say they are dying, but they talk about death more frequently. That is when your ears should be tuned in to their needs, not yours. She talked about what she wanted, from music to scripture, to wailers, yes, wailers, and what she wanted for her funeral. She especially wanted to invoke enough emotion that people would cry over the loss of her. Open casket, no pictures please.

As we sat in the living room she listened to the hum of my voice as I made small talk. We reminisced about the things she loved. She loved beautiful flowers. She would say, "Dress like a lady and you will be treated like a lady." She wanted to look elegant. No outfit was complete without gloves and a hat.

I laughed to myself about how she pronounced a "v" like a "w". Vacuum was a "wacuum" cleaner. She had taught me many things despite her many oddities, as I realized this may be my mom's last few months. All my siblings were too far away or too busy raising their own children and may not have even considered how seriously ill our mom was. But I saw her rapidly deteriorate on a daily basis.

One morning she was laying on the couch. I knew she was having memory issues. She would ask Felix for a certain kind of jam. When he would give it to her she would ask if he had something else. He would put the same jam she had in the refrigerator and then offer it back to her as the new requested jam. She seemed to be satisfied with that one. She began mixing up our names. She would call me Edna, Donna or another relative's name, but not Lorraine. When I would say, "It's me, Momma, Lorraine," she would respond with, "I thought you were busy." But that morning we were in the living room and she was laying on the couch. I sat beside her and read the newspaper. I sensed something was going on. Within a half hour, she asked me "Don't you have something else to do? Go to your office or something?" And I said, I did not need to go, but took her cue and left the room. After about five minutes I went back to check on her. I was horrified that she had fallen and was laying on the floor in the hall between my bedroom and the living room. I called out, "Mom! You had a stroke! I'm calling an ambulance!" She pursed her lips and although I could not hear a word, I clearly saw her look me in the eye and mouth, "No." The ambulance was there within minutes.

The ambulance attendants said she had suffered a heart attack. They were able to revive her and got her to Chula Vista Hospital.

I took my daughter-in-law, Vicky, Fred's wife, to see her, as she twisted and writhed, with the head jerking violently, on a ventilator. It was a horrible experience, and it was like she was trying to twist and writhe her way out of her own body. Even though the doctors said this was involuntary and she was in a coma, I knew why my mom did not want to be revived. That is probably why she mouthed, "No", when I said I was calling an ambulance. There was no such thing as a medical directive at the time, and because she came from out of state, we were required by law to keep her on a ventilator for 24 hours, to avoid a worse consequence of an inquest or perform an autopsy.

She did not want to be revived, and most certainly did not want to be on life support. She had told me these many times, as she recited what scripture she wanted, what songs to be sung and how many wailers she wanted. When I asked, "Why wailers, Momma?" she said, "I want lots of flowers and people to cry." I thought wailers would do the trick or just scare the hell out of everyone, like I had been when Mora would start wailing.

Vicky was terrified – spooked, in fact. I had insisted she see her own mother, as she was dying. Although Vickie spent her teenage years with the Fittro's as a foster child, she had a strained relationship with her own mother. But her mother died just before she and Fred got married. In the end, she knew why I insisted. But going with me was another thing. She loved Grandma but saying goodbye to what appeared to be an apparition was terrifying!

I tried to calm her down, and maybe myself too as I told her about my own dad's funeral. My mother had instructed us all to wear dark clothes, not to smile or laugh. "Be sad and act like your father just died!" she said. And we had to keep the flowers in the house from the day of his funeral, December 2, through the end of December. All those funerary pieces that belonged on a stand or a casket were dotted throughout our living room. Over the piano, next to the piano, on chairs, on the dining table, flowers all attested to the popularity or worth you were measured by. I can still conjure the acrid smell of those dying flowers and have made it abundantly clear that I wanted flowers while I was alive since that time.

When it was time to make that final call, I called my brother, Jim, to start the family hotline. My frail mom passed away quietly on May 1, coincidentally, Rod's 32nd birthday. She was laid to rest in Max, North Dakota, beside her husband, Isahiah "Sam" Samuel, without the wailers she had specifically requested. There were tears, but no wailing.

When a loved one passes away of course you miss them. Even though she lived her faith throughout her entire life though, there was some hesitation about the hereafter and where my mom would go after she died. And if you do not have a strong faith-based belief you may be wondering what happens too. Read John 3:16 for immediate instruction then call a friend to help you with this question. You will be comforted. When she was lying in bed the night before she had the fatal heart attack, she said, "I hope I get to Heaven." A lot of her faith was built on legalism and rules of denial.

Wikipedia describes legalism as a pejorative term that states in part that law is above gospel. The Encyclopaedia of Christianity states the same pejorative but adds the descriptor that it is the direct or indirect attachment of behaviours or disciplines to achieve one's salvation or standing before God. And to gain salvation you must perform certain deeds as opposed to actually believing in your own salvation through the grace of God that is given to you through your faith in Jesus Christ.

And boy did she have rules and beliefs. "Don't smoke or chew," "Don't drink," "Don't swear," "Don't be lazy," "Don't be stingy," "Don't gamble or play cards," "No dancing," "no secular entertainment (She apparently made an exception for the box social), "which had wide berth. Lots of don'ts and few dos. And most of all, be modest. Especially, wear a hat and gloves. She did not have the full understanding that once you accept Jesus Christ, He does not abandon you. Like my Aunt, I think my mom had lived alone too long. There were fears that I take for granted, even in my "senior" years now, that they both had been deeply bothered by. I do not worry or think about this because my joy has been in the journey and the deep faith and knowledge that I know this is not my final home, I am just a passing through.

I expressed what I know and believe about faith. That did not seem to comfort her and only confounded her. That prompted me to ask her how I knew for sure she was my mother. When she said, "I told you." I asked if this changes when she dies. "Of course not," she said. In that tender moment I was able to share the scripture that served as comfort to me over and over again, Hebrews 11:6, "And without faith it is impossible to please Him, for whoever would draw near to God must believe that He exists and that He rewards those who seek Him."

After we came back from my mother's funeral, we needed a new project to focus our grieving attention on. The next year kept us busy renovating and completing the conversion of the double garage into a useful apartment. I really thought this was where I would live if I needed to rent out the house for income. Little did I know this would become a second home to Walter, then James, and then finally, renters.

But first, Han enjoyed the quiet away from the house. Like leaving home, only not. Fred lived there a few months. Eventually Han took to the place like it was his new home. It gave him time to think about things. He came into breakfast one morning and announced that I would be going back to school to learn about electronics and computers. "Why?" I asked. "Because it is the future and you don't want to be left behind," was his response. I went to Southwestern College for a year, taking courses and learning. It is a lot harder to go back to school and learn something new as we get older. For me, it was overwhelming. It was not the intuitive computing today. I had to learn where F1 and F2 took you. Then put it on an external drive – called a floppy disc. Younger students ran circles around me until I finally got a private tutor so I could keep up. When I look back on it, the typewriter was my technology point of reference. The skills needed to learn the computing language was the distance from Earth to the moon for me.

Just six months shy of 60 I had been active with my painting and still teaching piano. It was probably a good thing I had a hobby that would keep me around the house. Although Han was not a hovering husband, he still needed to be checked in on. He had moved full time out to the newly completed apartment in the back and was busy puttering with the cactus garden and our dog. He was thorough about everything from books and records to making his final arrangements, right down to the last detail. In other words, all I had to do was make one call. When we got married, I thought maybe becoming a Christian would change his mind about cremation or at least having a memorial service. He did not want any of that. He wanted simplicity. In his own handwriting he handed me the Neptune Society certificate that said it all. Where I put his ashes was between me and his family.

Little did I know that Han had another reason for moving into the back apartment. He had been sick and probably knew this for some time but did not want me to know how sick he was - or that he had become his own doctor. After a year I noticed more and more that he was eating less and less. A doctor's visit confirmed he had congestive heart failure, but it was the stomach cancer that would take his life. Hospice was relatively new but what a gift it was. Being able to die with dignity is a dying person's real wish. And it is important to be tuned into this. Dutch had wanted to be home – and was until the last 24 hours. And even then, his trip to the hospital was solely to meet legal obligations and eliminate the unthinkable indignity of an autopsy, after suffering nine months with cancer.

One of the benefits of a second marriage is that you are more open about discussing things that might otherwise be slightly uncomfortable. We were past all that. Han was home and was on Hospice care. The one call was not even made by me, but was handled by his grandson, Dr. Steve, when that moment came. Although we had not seen Steven for a while, he coincidentally, but divinely intervened, the day Han passed. The blessing of not making that call was so timely and in the blink of an eye, Han was gone.

That was it, right? Or so I thought.

Death Certificates are needed for just about everything. I expected to pick those up with my husband's remains and was waiting for a phone call from the Neptune Society. After three weeks of waiting to close bank accounts, and for the insurance and retirement check to be put in my name, I called them to find out when I would get both my husband's remains and the death certificates.

"We're sorry, but we can't find his body."

"What? What do you mean you can't find him? He's dead. HE didn't go anywhere!"

"We're sorry ma'am, but we must have sent him to the wrong place."

"Dear God!" I exclaimed. "What does the wrong place mean? Where is he?"

The attendant was very apologetic but explained that maybe his body was sent to Los Angeles and that there must be a mix up. You think?

After some more apologies she said she would call back. Well, I certainly hope so.

After a few days I got a phone call from the Neptune Society exclaiming they had *found* my husband's remains and I should come in and retrieve them.

When I arrived, there was some additional scurrying and mumbling. Eventually a person at the front desk informed me that I would need to pay an additional $200 to receive the death certificate and remains.

"You've got to be joking! Where am I going to get $200, and why should I pay for something that was already prepaid?" I asked. They said there were additional costs in finding him. "That is not my problem," I said. "Why should I pay for your mistake?" "Well, we need payment in order to release the death certificates," they said. And that would be why I would have to give my cooperation, however reluctantly.

It was 1990 and you might as well have said $25,000. On a widow's yet-to-be-established pension, I would have to teach for 8 hours to get $200. So, I told them I would be back later in the day with a payment. I needed to get the death certificates to get the Railroad pension Han was receiving so I had to come up with the money. All the grumbling about their ineptness was not going to serve me. The questioning of, "Why me" or the hand wringing was not going to change the minds of these people, so I went home and broke the piggy bank open. Literally, I went to the bank, bought $20 worth of pennies and brought it in a bag and dropped it on Neptune's desk.

The look on their face was priceless. I told them I would make payments monthly. Faithfully, I brought $20 worth of pennies to them for the next nine months. It was not that I could not pay them all at one time. But I did not get the service that was prepaid so why should I give them another dime? I chose pennies instead.

Within days of the final payment, I received a notice from an attorney in the mail that the Neptune Society was being sued in a class action lawsuit. I did not have any idea what that meant and asked my daughter, Linda, to handle it. And boy did she. She wrote about her mother's disturbing and unnecessary angst over Neptune's losing the body of her husband, not knowing if what she received was even him (the toe tag had a number, not a name) and then the ensuing hustle for an additional $200.

In the end I received two times what Han prepaid, and the $200, in a check, fortunately not in pennies, back. It was a gift. I had not expected it. In fact, I thought, Han would want me to benefit from this. I used that money to pay down my car. Han would surely be happy and have a good laugh. Within a year of losing my mom, I lost my good and faithful friend. He was faithful to the end.

Losing a parent, spouse, or someone close to you is difficult. Even though death is inevitable it is harder if we do not have the faith and knowledge of where we are going after we die. I am at peace with my belief and am grateful to have had the opportunity to give that same peace of mind to my mother and two husbands before they died.

If you ever need that comfort of knowing what and where your faith is, Hebrews should be your go-to place. Does Hebrews know a thing or 270 about faith? In the NIV translation faith is mentioned 270 times. Faithful is used 83 times. Faithfully is used 18 times. Faithfulness gets used 59 times. Hebrews 11 gives the best examples of faith and meaning. The basic meaning of faith is trust and commitment in God.

Is faith really necessary to believe in God?

Author John Wright Follette wrote that for faith to be exercised, three things must be established.

First, Natural impossibility. It's the very place that faith exists and works. The object of our faith must be beyond our ability. Otherwise, human effort, not faith, could accomplish it.

Second, faith is hoped for through a yearning heart with a pure motive. That's why we call on the name of our Heavenly Father through our prayers in the name of Jesus Christ.

And third, your personal conviction about what you believe in and that it is as real as if it had already happened. In other words, you take it to the Lord in prayer and leave it there. Faith knows that God will deliver us.

This forms the basis or foundation of my belief. This has given me the confidence and assurance of my belief in God. To walk by faith means that my faith is working even though I cannot see how. That is not my job. My job is what, or what I call forth in my belief and prayer and through who, Jesus Christ, that will deliver this. The How part is God's.

He is faithful to the end.

The Brady Bunch Don't Live Here

When I was a child, I spoke as a child, I understood as a child, I thought as a child; but when I became a man, I put away childish things.

1 Corinthians 13:11 (KJ21)

Chapter 20

The Brady Bunch Don't Live Here

Growing up in the 60s and 70s, the small town of Imperial Beach was like any other small coastal town in San Diego County. The commonality of this small community such as norms, religion, values, customs, or identity was similar, except for one thing. There were more bars than churches than any other city in San Diego County.

It may be surprising that my own hometown of Max, North Dakota, despite its small population, had 5 churches and 7 bars. We would consider them "dives" today, but back then it was a place to shoot some pool, the breeze, and congregate, especially if you did not belong to a church. If you were a member of a church, your fellowship was *not* found in the local bar.

Looking back on my own childhood, my dad made his own beer in the basement, and maintained a "mini bar" in the sitting room of our boarding house my parents ran at Devil's Lake, during prohibition. It was more like a modified speak-easy because the locals were there more frequently than the guests we housed. Guests were mostly employees of the railroad and just needed some shut eye before boarding a train coming through the next morning. This seemed as normal to me in North Dakota as it did to me in San Diego.

We loved our four miles of beach stretching from the mouth of the Tijuana River to the pristine beaches of Coronado strand. Views of long waves stretching as far as the eye could see and rolling long waves to shore, I could not imagine myself on any other shore. And why would I? This is what drew us here and has kept me here all these years. We marveled at all the helicopters flying overhead as we headed outside and went about our business. Today it is a little noisier with the jets screaming their power of the air to monitor our borders. Top Gun schools draw attention worldwide.

The confluence of military presence in San Diego County created the trifecta of Naval power on and under the sea and in the air. Imperial Beach represents the location for the tail of this power, hosting as it still does today, Ream Field. In the 60's this was the largest helicopter base in the world. Just a few miles up the strand, past the sand dunes, the Navy SEALs training facility established their beachhead on January 1, 1962, at the command of President Kennedy. We used to drive up the strand to Coronado and go to the State Beach Park, or into town to one of the new restaurants. Coronado is still a destination location.

At the end of Coronado, North Island Naval base, home port to several aircraft carriers, still maintains a major presence. As Palm Avenue ends the Strand begins. We would drive past this behemoth but odd-looking cage the locals called the elephant cage. We knew it was on military land, but we had no idea what it functioned as. The kids would make up stories about this thing being used to communicate with aliens, and I must admit we went along with some fabrication of our own. But the Wullenweber Circular Disposed Antennae Array stood since 1965 until 1999. Essentially a big circular antenna, the direction finder was a primary communication link for US Navy submarines.

With the removal of that antennae, the Navy commissioned the new $1.2 B Navy SEAL training complex (Silver Strand Training Complex South), consisting of 44 buildings, starting from where that antenna used to be and ending at the NW side of Imperial Beach.

Being sandwiched between Ream Field, now called the Naval Outlying Landing Field, just two blocks from my home, and the south gate of the training facility, the additional 3,000 personnel by 2021 is not the Imperial Beach of the 60', 70s, 80s, 90s and even the first decade of this century.

According to the 1960 census there was a total population of 17,773. Maybe due to the transient nature of the military or lack of progress due to the NIMBY (not in my backyard) city council, development was slow and construction even slower. This little town seemed like a place time had forgotten. Even by 2019 approximation, the total population appears to be roughly 40% higher than the 1960 census. With the new SEAL Training complex, that growth stunt is now a bygone era.

Back then, these three original strategic Naval locations were in various stages of preparing or departing for an unpopular war in Vietnam. Little did we know that this military sleeping giant awoke to take a very large presence in our little town of Imperial Beach. By 1965, over 82,000 troops were in Vietnam with another 175,000 preparing to leave. It was not just the Navy that enlisted or recruited.

Young men recruited to the Marines, departing anywhere west of the Mississippi, came to San Diego, where they were processed at the Marine Corp Recruit Depot (MCRD) at 32nd Street. From there they were sent to the 350+ plus acre training facility at Camp Pendleton in north county San Diego. Through rigorous training young men were transformed into mean lean fighting machines. Today it transforms over 21,000 men and women annually.

Much of the country did not even know where Vietnam was let alone Imperial Beach. Now we were involved in this foreign war, and it began to take on a more sinister meaning. Not since WWII had there been a draft, but each month the military needed more personnel, and the draft was reinstituted. The draft created deep fear and mistrust. Being drafted meant going overseas, to fight an invisible enemy, and maybe not even returning home alive. By 1967 over 500,000 troops were in Vietnam as anti-war protests mounted.

My own church started to change too. Some young men had already enlisted and were serving a first and even second tour of duty. As more recruits arrived in San Diego some looked for a new church body and found their way to Calvary Baptist. Fears of my own sons going to war increased too. Fred, Sam, and Rod talked with the military and draft age guys at the church. They wanted no part of this war and began to talk about their options. Fred was going to go to college, Sam was going to go to Canada.

The war played out on nightly television as many fatalities, injured and broken-winged men came back from duty. With the increasing conflict on foreign soil, the conflict in the US grew. "One-two-three what are we fighting for" lyrics heard at this obscure sounding concert called Woodstock in 1968 became the war chant of the draft age men.

With enlistments down, the draft was even more unpopular. On Dutch's 47th birthday, November 26, 1969, President Nixon issued an executive order of random selection or the draft lottery. The odds that one or 3 of my draft-aged sons would be drafted increased significantly. I was not opposed to their service. I was opposed to losing my sons in a war no one understood, and fatalities were high. You bet I prayed hard.

Rod was drafted in the third selection. His entrance to college would defer his status if he was progressing in college. Rod became my only son to graduate college. He would serve if he had to, but college spared him. I thank God for this miracle that Rod would go on to have a family of his own and spared serving in Vietnam duty.

Imperial Beach, or IB as the locals call it, is geographically desirable to the Naval facilities, and until recently was one of the most affordable places to live in San Diego. Prior to the Coronado Bay bridge's 1969 completion, the only way to Coronado Island was over a car ferry from downtown San Diego or through Imperial Beach. There are still only two thoroughfares for cars to IB, which may explain the sense of isolation from the rest of the world.

Without the distraction of cell phones, video games or social media, growing up in Imperial Beach seemed an ideal place to raise kids. Before and after school activities were surfing, sports or a part time job. It never occurred to me how easy it was to access your vice of choice. Cigarettes were the easiest. You could go to the Palm Theatre, drop $.25 or $.35 for premium cigarettes into a vending machine that dispensed your favorite brand. No ID. Underage drinking was even easier. One of the boys could have one of the numerous young military guys buy their booze and there was no legal consequence. Being at the border, drugs were smuggled in on a regular basis, something I would be personally impacted by throughout my teenage boys' years and into their adulthood. Dealing with this was like playing whack-a-mole. Choose your battle. Triage the worst.

As a parent you do everything you can to prevent access to these moral harms. It had been long established what alcohol does to an adult, and I was dealing with this in my own home. What impact this would have on my sons was not yet known. Instinctively I knew that keeping the kids busy with as many church activities as possible, only went so far. Music did not interest the boys as much as it did Linda and Rod. My hands were full.

So, does parenting stop when the kids have grown up and left home? No. You just have less influence, and your choice of when to speak up narrows. You never stop being a parent.

Adult kids do not hear your advice any more than they did as a teenager. They just ask more because they are now more aware of the consequences you warned them about.

It Really Did Take A Village

Remember your leaders, who
spoke the word of God to
you. Consider the outcome of
their way of life and
imitate their faith.

Hebrews 13:7 (NIV)

228

Chapter 21

It Really Did Take a Village

At almost 90, I laugh that the lines have blurred between the sound of my mother's advice and my own. Gone since 1985, I still hear her words as they come out of my mouth. More contextual and contemporary, my values and ethics were shaped by my parents more than anyone. This is my core.

When the kids were growing up, I relied on the eyes and ears of the community to help me raise them. It took a village. Sometimes a piano student saw one of them doing something, even a storekeeper. By the time the kids got home I would ask a presumptive question, as if I already knew what they'd been up to. Sitting on the piano bench at the front of the church gave me an eyeful but sometimes a parent would tell me that one of mine had walked off with one of theirs and ditched the services. On one or two occasions a police officer brought one of them home. Thinking back on that, the anticipation of being delivered back to me was probably worse, in their minds, than being in the back of the cruiser. At least when they were younger. Then, the anticipation of "wait till your dad gets home", then lectured by both parents, lose freedom then get watched like a hawk was torture to them. This was decades before cell phones so restriction, or more alone time with your parents, should be avoided at all costs.

Despite wanting the best for them, typically teenagers and young adults want little or no advice from parents to craft their lives. Mine were no exception. It may be natural, but it was a battle of wit and will and more "you will" and not theirs, which caused a lot of conflict.

While writing this chapter my eldest, Fred, revealed drinking for him and Sam started in junior high. Easy access. Beer and cigarettes gave way to thrill seeking as they began experimenting with more substances.

It astounds me that no matter how young, bad influence can be monitored but not stopped by ordering it so. But how did I not know this? Access to beer and cigarettes was apparently as easy as getting a half gallon of milk. Access to drugs was easier, done under the cloak of darkness and hidden from sight.

Suspecting your child was under the influence of something, you had little but your senses to rely on. The only middle-class option to sending your child to a relative's was to sign them up for military duty. So, it was shoot from the lip and keep asking questions. In other words, stay calm and keep firing.

As they got better at dodging, I had to pick my battles carefully. This child rearing phase was even taken to our minister Rev Gates at Calvary Baptist Church. He advised the more I held tight the more they would fight. "Let go and let God" would have to become my new mantra. There were many books from birth order to Dr Spock, all advising the best way to raise your child.

I skipped all that. Spare the rod and spoil the child, albeit tempting, wasn't an option either since it was a 1600 poem on corporal punishment, by Samuel Butler.

My child rearing was based on common sense and reliance on Proverbs 22:6, "Raise up the child in the way he should go. When he is old, he will not depart in it." And Ephesians 6:4, "Fathers do not provoke your children to anger by the way you rule them. Rather bring them up with the discipline and instruction that comes from the Lord."

It's interesting that Mother is not instructed in this verse but it's our obligation and responsibility too. But what if the child provoked the parent through their rebellious and unacceptable behavior? Was I just supposed to just pray about it? I was obviously conflicted, but my last nerve was shattered. I didn't stop praying though. I resolved to pray more. But the more I prayed, the more I was challenged, and this is often the case in our walk with God. I prayed for the challenges to stop but as they continued, I thought, "Maybe I have this prayer backwards." Instead, I started thanking God for the challenges and my outlook began to improve.

Early on Sam was my rebel that I hoped would grow out of his risky behavior. Lauren was my next rebel, who had come to date a satanic worshipper. Sam was the second son; Lauren was the second daughter. Maybe there was something to this birth order idea.

Rod and Linda had aspirations of their own. They would go off to college and finish what they started. Fiercely independent, I didn't worry about their choices. James had served a tour of duty and was trying to make sense of marriage a few times. If Del was into anything I would never find out. He would get a challenge of his own when he overcame and conquered a life-threatening illness in his 30's.

As they became adults, I saw them less as they busied themselves with their own lives. Or maybe I was a little afraid to look too close at their adult behavior. But as they became adults their problems elevated until they too had to deal with them. As adults, they come with their problems, needs, challenges, and yes, thankfully, victories. Each problem was as different as each child, and no one size fits all advice either. What applied to one did not to another. Having 9 kids gave me a real insight to early childhood development, for which I was an expert now.

Parenting is lifelong.

When Han passed Fred came home, who had been dealing with his own parenting problems and outgrowth of his divorce. He'd only been home a few months when I announced I was going to see my youngest sister in Canada and, "Would he like to go?"

Without the responsibilities of marriage or someone to take care of I was no longer responsible to answer to anyone on how I spent my time. That can be just as freeing as it is confounding with what to do with yourself. If you are not careful you can fall into despair, which starts innocently as a pity party. I have many friends today, even relatives that are far more interested in their problems than a solution. I have learned to be a sounding board only so far. If you don't set a boundary, you have none, and their problems become yours as they intertwine you in them.

I channeled my energy into something more productive by working and traveling, which was more rewarding.

When I got ready to leave Canada, Fred stayed. Within a month, however, he found himself in hot water. Thinking it was the right thing to do, he sought a work visa after he had started working. Canadian immigration told him he had to leave. Dwayne, who had moved to Idaho, picked Fred up on the US/Canada border in Montana, no longer welcome in Canada.

Dwayne's then continued avoidance of his 5 DUIs had caught up with him. After serving his obligations with the State of California he went to Idaho and started over. It was time for a change for them. Slowly Dwayne was joined by Fred, then nephew Jason, then Del Jr. Eventually Del would bring Sam, who was 100% engaged in the riskiest lifestyle of all and had to be lulled off a mountain in San Diego overlooking the US/Mexican border. No kidding this isn't the Brady Bunch of 70's television.

Starting over seemed to be catchy. I had also determined that I would not sit idly by, and watch life happen to everyone else. So, my credit card and I boarded a plane and headed for Europe. Landing in England the cities were as fascinating as the countryside, but the white cliffs of Dover are as marvelous as the lyrics that were written about them. I studied the art I saw in as many museums as we went into. Crossing the English Channel; traveling to Normandy, then the tidal miracles of Mt St Michel, and French countryside eventually took us through the lavender fields of southern France. I fell in love with traveling. We continued to Italy. Seeing the Sistine Chapel was a dream come true. I couldn't imagine standing on that scaffolding for years to paint the frescoes though, any more than understanding that the Vatican was its own country. Seeing history through the eyes and ears of the guides made the gladiator's chariot races come alive.

We travelled up the Rhine to the Seine and saw much of Germany's meticulous hillside grooming and German efficiency. Stopping in Munich I even got a chance to meet a cousin from the Bokovoy clan. Traveling in the clean and big Mercedes Benz busses, we marveled at the tour guide's extensive knowledge of history, mixed with humor and odd facts. I loved Venice, the Alps and even Hitler's hiding spot, the Eagle's Nest, but Vienna was my favorite spot. We headed back to Paris and got off our tour. Visiting the Louvre two times wasn't enough. But after a month on the road my exhausted credit card longed for a break. Come to think of it, I longed for my own shower and of course a good night's sleep in my own bed and I gladly went home.

My art trade picked up and I was busy with art shows and commissioned pieces while trying to remember and sketch as many things as possible I had seen on my trip. I was at peace with being alone. And I certainly wasn't lonely.

Good grief, the kids came and went, and I was grateful they were figuring out things on their own. What I had learned was that the more you fix their problems, the more you will fix their problems and they don't learn how to.

In the period of a year, though, it seemed that everyone that had been married at the time was getting divorced. Sam and Laurie, who had become Lauren by this time, had already divorced. Rod was the only one that married for life.

One afternoon while I was in the art studio, I got a call from my son, James who was living in Livonia, Michigan with his second wife and her two daughters and their two sons. With a daughter from his previous marriage, in Washington, and a son in New York, he had settled in Michigan to begin acquiring culinary skills that would lead to better paying jobs in high end restaurants.

He sounded upset and distracted. He said he had some bad news and that his wife, Pam, who was coming home from work late the previous night, had been in an accident and was killed. His voice softened as he said her family wanted to keep the kids together including the boys. "What would you do," he asked. "I would fight to keep my kids," I said. "That's what I was hoping you would say. Can I come back home?"

When you receive this kind of news you sometimes only have a few minutes to figure out the right things to say but seconds to decide. In my heart I knew this was the right decision. There have been more adult children moving back home to live with their parents in the past two decades than there has ever been. But then it was less common.

With my rental unit vacant I said, "I'll help you with the kids, but I won't raise them." He promised me this would work, and he moved in. From that moment on there was limited free time and I found myself absorbed in their 7- and 9-year-old lives as I ferried them to school, the zoo and church. Within eight months, James made good on his promise and got back on his feet financially, moving on. My taxying and teaching them piano went on for a few more years. By then John and Jeff were wearing out my shock absorbers. As a grandparent it was hard to watch the choices they would eventually make.

Fred moved back to San Diego and with his help I continued to take the boys to church and influenced them in the best way I knew how. Initially Fred lived in the back apartment, which by that time was getting a lot of use. Clearly if it takes a village, and we were the original village people.

Lauren had remarried and she and Linda were pregnant about the same time with baby girls of their own, within 6 months of each other.

It was so odd, but as a mother of 9 that had babies sequentially one year after another, with very few breaks, that being a grandparent would be so spread out. After 81 months of my own pregnancies, over a thirteen-year period, or 144 months, this meant that most of those months were spent changing diapers.

My children took more time to have children, as if they had all the time in the world. The first grandchild, Jason, was born in 1972 to Sam and Julie, to the last one, Alena, in 1995 to Linda and Eric. But grandparenting comes with privilege, including the option to change diapers.

Fred and Vickie had Jennifer, Matthew and Courtni, within their first five years. Sam and Julie had Jason and Shauna within a few years of marriage. That is, after a surprise visit before Sam got married, from a young woman introducing us to what she said was our grandchild. Although we were never able to conclude the legitimacy of this claim there are many ways today to determine the rightful origin of this child. And she deserves that. At 90, I would welcome another grandchild. But you 'd better hurry!

Am I done being a parent? Apparently not.

In late November 1998 Walter moved home. Everyone called him Wally, Walligator and the great Waldo Pepper. He was Walter to me. He had responded to an ad to rent to buy a house with his girlfriend. After doing all the remodeling and construction work, the dilapidated house looked pretty good and they were proud of their work. The owner thought so too. Suddenly claiming there wasn't a viable contract, he evicted them to get the house back.

Walter said moving back would be temporary. How temporary would not be revealed to me for several months. It was a surprise and a joy to have him home. He had an adventurous spirit and an easy smile. He had a wicked sense of humor and would bring his friends in the house to tease me and have fun. He mentioned an itch in his arm he couldn't seem to scratch but that didn't stop him from buying a boat and spending free time fishing.

After a few months Walter asked if he could store another boat in the yard. It belonged to "friends" of his and I said, "No." This used Zodiac, on its own trailer, showed up in the yard. I made sure as soon as it showed up that this boat got off my property.

Little did I know this boat would lead to Walter's downfall. Like my former piano students that would come to me innocently and tell me that one of my kids was doing something, I started hearing rumors that Walter was hanging out with the wrong crowd. I started asking him questions. Where there is smoke, there is fire. The more I asked the more I learned.

I would eventually, but after the fact, come to learn this boat was not used for fishing. It was used for smuggling. Walter and his good friend Gino had gotten caught up in the easy and fast lifestyle of a smuggling operation that they were lookouts for. The "friends" used this boat to bring drugs from Mexico onto the IB beach we had frequented as a family. Under the silence of a dark night Walter and Gino would watch out and communicated with the operation by walkie talkie. It is still inconceivable to me that by his own admittance, this drug ring had operated undetected for several years. That is, until one dark night.

Please God, not now!

Overlook my youthful sins, O Lord!
Look at me instead through eyes of
mercy and forgiveness, through eyes
of everlasting love and kindness.

Psalm 25:6 (TLB)

Chapter 22

Please God, Not Now!

Walter was sitting in a van on the bay side of the strand. He was near the private marina and waiting for a signal from one of the guys in this group, who had gone to the beach side of Silver Strand to meet the arriving pontoon. The cohort's signal would tell Walter to come get him and the cargo that was being unloaded onshore.

Instead, Walter saw 2 police helicopters spotlights and the flashing lights and sirens of fast approaching police cars descending on the very site he was about to drive into. Abandoning plans, and the van, he quietly walked to a nearby bus bench, miraculously taking the infrequent approaching bus away from the scene. I never really knew what had happened back then.

Thirty years later, as bits and pieces of information have been revealed I have finally put this puzzle together today but for years this haunted me. Walter was my dearly loved baby boy that had a hard time surviving when he was two. We had a unique and special bond that was different from any of my children. He had fought to live but now he was fighting to be free.

When your child gets in trouble do you abandon him or her?

The answer was easy for me.

For you, the reader, it may be a mixed bag. If you have had a lifetime of rescuing your child, you may feel differently because you have been so manipulated and lied to that you're burned out. But even if that is true that spark of hope lives deep within a mother. The flame never goes out.

Like Job, you may feel like your heart is full of the boils he had, and say, "I'm done." And like Job, those words may take root. His trials may have only lasted nine months, but they were horrendous trials he would never forget.

You may feel the same as Job and have even had years of trials. But like Job, who said, "I know my Redeemer lives," he believed God would deliver him and defeated what seemed impossible and God did deliver him, blessing him with more than he could have ever imagined.

Thankfully, even when we stray from our foundation, our Heavenly Father welcomes us back with open arms. And if your prodigal child turns to you for forgiveness, give it without reserve. You may not see a way, but my belief in God encourages and rewards me to believe there is a way. That is the rock of my belief and the foundation of hope, faith and trust.

To put this in perspective, my husband's oldest sister had three children. One died in her teens of non-Hodgkin's lymphoma. She fought every day of her life from the first diagnosis to live one more day until the last day she lived. Her younger sister in contrast outlived her at least fifteen or twenty years and chose a hard life that would have killed most people within a year. Her drug of choice was heroin. For years, her mother and only brother were tortured by her lifestyle. She would cry, promise to change, and eventually stole her mother's trust and faith in her. But my sister-in-law never gave up hope. Before she died, she and her son probably had some tough discussions that a dying parent has just before passing the torch of their life to the next generation.

Candy moved to Los Angeles and was within 5 miles of Linda, but she never made contact and tried to get clean. She was. For a while. Then, one more use at the same dose she had previously taken before she got clean, took her out. The next time her brother would see her was to identify her. The seeming death wish she lived life by delivered its final blow. But it did not have to end this way. Her addiction was bigger than the reason to live.

What makes your child turn away from the values you raised them with and instead chooses a life that will only give them despair, and you, heartache? Whatever lesson we are learning, requires us to lean in and trust that God reveals His plan to us. That means you must stop listening to the negative voice that is always present. Receive what God says and get in agreement with God.

Walter wept and sought my forgiveness. He wanted and needed help. His friends had turned on him to lessen their sentences and after years of surveillance this closely-knit group of 8 had been infiltrated by an informer. Pictures and other evidence never placed Walter at the scene of the crime, but he was known and in the line of fire. His cooperation stopped there. He took the fall to protect another risk-seeking sibling. That sibling may not have been involved with the main operation, but he was still complicit. Walter took the hit.

Before all of this happened, I continued to live the same modest lifestyle I always had. We were middle class by any standard unless and until one step away from a total disaster. As I thought about the legal battle that did not ensure he would walk free I had to balance this with how I could help without "breaking the bank."

In 1998, as an accomplice, he had a $1,000,000 bail. $100,000 was my limit and I posted bail with a note on the house that was worth $300,000 at the time. It was never a question and I'd do it again.

Walter walked on eggshells, hoping to avoid the worst sentence that would send him to a prison for years. The stress was unbelievable.

Trying to make life seem normal under these circumstances required a lot of prayer and distractions to keep my mind off the inevitable. That's God's way of keeping us from falling into despair. My eldest son, Fred, was starting a new life with a bride that would become his best decision to make a great future together possible. On his and Deborah's marriage all my children, Sam, Rod and Elizabeth, Linda and then husband Dan, James, Lauren and husband Marc were there except Del and Walter.

Del did not like spending money and a second marriage for his older brother did not make any sense to him, especially when he had never married once. But Walter could not attend. Instead of sharing a family celebration Walter had to attend a required class or be in contempt of court.

Friday morning, after a few days of enjoying the family celebration, I had scheduled some routine maintenance to be done on the house. Before the carpets could be cleaned, I needed the potted plants moved outside. I could not move them, so I called Walter in to help.

"Yeah Ma, I'll be right there," he said. He came in, moved the plants and I went back inside. I forgot I had something in the living room to move so I went back outside to ask him to help me. As he followed me back in the house, I heard him make a strange noise and I turned around and I was now looking at him prone on the ground. My head raced and my heart pumped madly till I felt it pounding in my ears.

Instinctively acting, I raced to him and held him in my arms as I called out to anyone that could hear me. A mother's call from the soul can be heard by anyone.

You may have experienced this or even heard of someone that has told you they felt something and could not explain it. A hunch, a sensation or even premonition that something is wrong or a sudden desire to call a person. It is called Divine Intervention. I believe that we are not meant to face the many challenges of life alone, even if we are. So, listen to the still small voice, or the coincidental timing of a phone call or billboard with a message only you understand. That's God and the many messengers used to tell you something.

Time is a blur, but I called 911 and someone at the church to start a prayer chain. As I held him in my arms, Walter died as paramedics arrived. I begged God to please spare him one more time. "Give me one more day with him," as I sobbed my love into his face. "One miracle…please," and prayed for a miracle as the paramedics hovered over Walter's still body. I found myself saying, "Please God, not now! He's only 36."

Paramedics were able to revive him and raced him to Chula Vista Hospital. There, they were unable to sustain him, and my dear and wonderful baby boy died.

Some people find it hard to believe in the coincidence of divine intervention. Especially the officers that were prepared to pick Wally up and take him voluntarily to prison. They even attended his memorial service in total disbelief, thinking Walter must have faked his own death to avoid a prison sentence.

As of this writing I think of the time his 1st grade teacher told me he had thrown a handful of rice, in a class exercise about Hawaii, across the room, saying, "Welcome to the islands!" It amuses me to think that Walter may be on a great big boat, fishing on some heavenly island, biding his time. But back then it was salt in a wound and I was deeply wounded.

Grief-stricken with the last thing a parent should ever have to do, I turned my attention to burying him. With limited funds I now freely gave up my own plot next to my husband at Polson Cemetery in Montana.

As I made burial arrangements it was important to me that I was on the same plane leaving San Diego as Walter. I was assured by the airlines that this was possible. Coordinating our arrival, all arrangements were made, including meeting Linda and Lauren in Salt Lake City on a connection to continue our journey together.

As we stood, utterly devastated, we silently watched out the window as cargo was loaded from the plane from San Diego to our connecting flight. Linda glanced out again and said, "Mom, I think that is Walter on the tarmac, next to the plane." I was relieved and said, "OK, Let's board now."

It was early morning, and the weather was good, so we did not expect any delays and arrived in Missoula on time. We rented a car to take us the hour and fifteen-minute drive to Polson. The mortuary met the plane and would take Walter on his final journey. When we arrived at the cemetery, we met the rest of the family and waited for the hearse. After an hour or so we started wondering what was taking them so long to arrive. Someone went into the mortuary office to find out what was taking so long, where we learned Walter was not on that flight at all!

Recalling the experience with Han's remains being lost for weeks, I became very anxious that a similar fate had occurred, and Walter's body was 'lost' too. We learned that he was left in the same place we had seen him, on the tarmac, back in Salt Lake City.

Finally, after a few hours he was delivered and buried.

There is a blessing here. It was plain as day. Walter would not be serving time here, but in the hereafter.

When we got back home Linda wrote a letter to the airlines. Tasking them with putting themselves in the shoes of a grieving mother that thought she was accompanying her son on his final journey, only to find out he had been deliberately left on a tarmac. Why, this must be an intentional infliction of emotional distress. She must have thought she was back in law school or writing her closing statement being deliberated in front of a jury, but she was a woman on a mission. Despite my telling her to just drop it she pursued them till they finally sent a plane ticket, all-expense paid, to anywhere I wanted. It was like Walter saying, "Welcome to the Islands, Ma!"

What lesson was I continuing to learn?

Do not talk yourself out of favor. When you are in a state of shock or grief it can be hard to see a blessing as God's favor. God's blessing is Divine Favor that takes you where you cannot go on your own.

If Jesus could find favor with a group of the oddest men put together, He puts you in situations you could not find on your own if you tried. What did a tax collector, a scribe, carpenter, and fishermen have in common? God saw favor in them.

In the same way, God finds favor in us through our lessons, so be open to accepting them. He turned my sorrow to peace.

Loss Has A Lesson About Forgiveness

He heals the brokenhearted and binds up their wounds.

Psalms 147:3 (NIV)

246

Chapter 23

Loss Has a Lesson About Forgiveness

To choose joy over sorrow requires a lot of faith.

It was the second week of December as I watched the lights twinkle on the trees and felt the crispness in the air of this time of year as we headed home. My daughter-in-law, Deborah and I were on our way back from seeing a Christmas performance. While she drove, I was reflecting on the visit I'd had with my 3rd son, Rod a few weeks earlier. I had joined my daughter Lauren and her husband Marc and their family in Ventura for Thanksgiving that year. While we were there, she said she wanted to see her brother and called him and told him we were coming to visit. After some discussion Rod said there was no reason to drive to Santa Barbara and he and his wife would meet us in Ventura within the hour.

After they arrived, he asked me to take a walk with him, as his wife stayed behind. I could see he was greatly disturbed and saw this as a confirmation of marital trouble. As we walked, he began to talk. As he talked, he began to open up, and speak about the pain he felt inside. He did not mix words and got to the point. He didn't feel like he was good enough, and that the family he married into did not accept him, called him a loser. He began to apologize that he had not been a better son and had not done enough for me. I started to cry with him as he continued to apologize that he had not brought his two children to visit more often. I knew how much he was hurting but I could not figure out what the root of the pain was. I had enjoyed seeing him for the family reunion several months earlier but wondered why he arrived with only his daughter. Then, I did not question him about his relationship with his wife but suspected that there was trouble. He wasn't happy and each time I started to ask him about it back then, I would change my mind. But now, I had to finally ask him what was wrong. Was his marriage in trouble?

If I could carry him under my heart for nine months, it was not a leap to say that as his mother I always knew when something was bothering him or any of my children. To respect his family's privacy, part of this conversation has been omitted. He began to weep. He said he had done something wrong, and "E" would not forgive him. When I asked what he'd done he would not say. As many times as I guessed, "Did you kill someone?" "No." "Was it infidelity?" He said "No". I told him that whatever happened we would help him. Did he need a loan? Again, he said, "No," and that he would work it out. Abruptly he said he had to go. Before he left, we prayed together, as we clung and wept.

As we were going back home Lauren said she was worried about Rod. She had never seen him so depressed. As I mulled these things over in my mind, I had not either. I did not realize how much I had been in deep thoughts as Deborah pulled into her driveway. Because of the hour, as I walked in, I thought, "How odd. Why is Sam at Fred's house?" It was after 7 in the evening, and I came into their house for fellowship and to share our joy of the evening's events.

"No! No, please tell me this isn't true, Fred!" as the words came swiftly out of his mouth that Rod had taken his life.

No words can ever express what I felt. My heart was broken. Tears came easily as we all wept.

The deeper the pain, the fewer words can be spoken.

I needed to go home. I was told Linda had received the call. She always said Rod was her emotional twin. She'd gone to Lauren's house, at the same time Fred and Sam were together to tell me, to tell her sister of this great loss. I called Linda.

She had hosted a birthday party for Lauren the night before. She told me she was cleaning up and putting up Christmas decorations. With the sound of Christmas carols on the radio the phone rang. As Linda turned down the music, she picked up the phone. "Hullo?" She did not recognize the voice on the other side of the phone. It was just before 2pm and the man's voice said he was the Presbyterian minister of Rod's church, explaining that he'd been asked by Rod's wife to call. "What? Why didn't Rod call me?" she asked. "I'm sorry Linda, but Rod took his life this morning." She asked many questions as he answered them. After a long silence he said, "There is something else. Rod's wife has requested that you respect her privacy and that your family not contact her."

I reached out to my pastor, Rev. Ted Selgo and his wife Susan, who helped me process this pain. I spent many hours in prayer and in my Bible for solace. Jesus knew my despair and brought favor through the kindness of friends, family and my church. The entire church was so good to me and provided me with the support that only a church body can. As much of a blur as his funeral was, I was grateful that my pastor and his wife, all my children and brother, Jim, were there.

Rod was a loving father who deeply loved his son and daughter, but his heart was broken. Not being able to measure up to the standards he lived with was devastating, and left him a hopeless broken man. In a momentary wave of despair, he took his life.

The theme song from M A S H, says suicide is painless. That may be, but not for the survivors of it.

We were later told that "Rod was sick" and allegedly a suicide prevention intervention had been planned that morning by Rod's best friend. I will never understand why it took so long to see Rod's despair, act or never ask us to help. That was brutal. But what I continue to learn is the act of forgiveness itself. Psalms 147:3, He heals the broken hearted and binds up their wounds. I continue to go to that verse even today.

When tragedy strikes it becomes a part of your journey, part of your life's message. You must go within and ask for God's protection from the voices you hear in your head. "I would have, I should have, why didn't I?" That is when you put it in God's hands, now go wash yours of it.

This does not mean it instantly stops and you magically no longer hurt. It means do not "what if," no matter how hard that is, and trust God that your heart will be healed. It also meant that I had to forgive. Forgive the act; forgive myself and especially forgive those that could, should, or would have helped.

We will not be able to handle the pain unless we believe and understand that there is a purpose. But what purpose could there be for this? To show Rod that he was loved and deeply cared for was only part of it. To learn to love beyond what we could see, hear or feel was another lesson. There would be more.

Just to be clear, the Bible does not offer a painless path to your life here on earth. From the many stories I have used as illustrations in this book you see one struggle after another with life. But it does offer us meaning and hope – and that is what has enabled me to deal with this unbearable pain.

Rick Warren, pastor of the Saddleback church in Orange County, California, spoke about the four stages of recovery from suicide he expressed in dealing with his own sorrow after his son's suicide.

At first, we are in shock, a human emotion. Wanting this to be over or wanting this to not be, so we deeply long for this grief to pass and wonder if we will ever get back to being normal.

Then sorrow, which he describes as a godly emotion in his illustration that, "Jesus wept." With the Bible declaring that we are made in His image, we grieve, as God surely grieves over what He sees us do.

Then struggle. This is when the "why" questions come up. For me it was, "Why didn't I." If you do not understand something's broken, it will not get fixed.

Then surrender. I had to be willing to surrender my will to His. I surrender all. I lost my son, that is true. But I surrendered my hurt and all to God. That was my salvation. All the questions answered required a walk with God and a belief that His Holy Spirit would comfort me. That through Jesus Christ, I would see my son again, and walk with him in Heaven. Rod was broken, but even a broken tree can bear fruit. His two beautiful children are leading productive and meaningful lives.

What was my lesson? If you see something, say something. Do not sit and watch your loved one suffer. Or think this is a phase and they will just get over it.

They will not voluntarily seek help because they do not see the dark coat of illness, they are wearing that is covering their pain or clouding their judgement. They cannot see what you see, and need help. If the loved one does not want your help, then enlist your mother, his mother, your brothers, your sister, his sister, the pastor, their friends, an army. Because life is in the balance of what you do next. And you cannot, must not give up on them. The point is don't just do nothing. Not being heard is the same as being silent.

If you are reading this and have thought of or are feeling suicidal

Help is available

Speak with someone today

National Suicide Prevention Lifeline

Hours: Available 24 hours.

800-273-8255

WWW.SURVIVORSOFSUICIDE.COM

The purpose of the Survivors of Suicide (SOS) website and program is to help those that have lost a loved one to suicide resolve their grief and pain in their own personal way. Grief that survivors of suicide experience are unique. If you have lost someone and are grieving, the questions often left behind can be unbearable. Grieving with others that have had a similar loss can help you get closure.

ARE YOUR PROBLEMS REALLY YOUR OWN FAULT?

But you do not know what will happen tomorrow! Your life is like a mist. You can see it for a short time, but then it goes away.

James 4:14 (ICB)

Chapter 24

Are Your Problems Really Your Own Fault?

Sometimes life offers you a second chance… It's called tomorrow. For the fortunate they've finally recognized a change must occur, or they will perish by their own will or choices. But for some, tomorrow may only be today, right now.

If you are given a second chance, recognize it as a gift of God's mercy. Second chances are not just for the individual. The second chance can be in a marriage that was unfaithful or broken. Even harsh words or distrust that broke down a relationship with a loved one or a business partner can happen, and snap! And just like that, the last straw breaks the proverbial camel's back.

Family relationships can be stretched to the breaking point too. You give and give and give till you are empty. You pray harder. You continue to pray your loved one back to health. But through their free will and choices made under the veil of an addiction, that loved one can and will choose to see no wrong until they hit bottom. For some this means the choice to change is a better one than death. For others the chronic choice brings about the inevitable.

As a parent, you never give up hope, but you do get tired of the reasons, the excuses, the life choices, the promises to change, the explanations, the effect it has on the other family members. And when 'they' get caught up in these stories, which is all about them, they have no concept of God, their loved ones or even think about how you hurt, or how much pain it causes. They have lost touch with reality, even humanity. They may talk about a relationship with God, but they do not know the power of God's might because they will not bend their will to His, and do not want to. They have reached the dysfunction junction.

Every second a seeker can start over is a remarkable gift because their life's choices and mistakes become initial drafts and, thankfully, not the final version.

When God is not the center of your universe you are serving two masters, which we know is not possible.

Matthew 6:24 (NIV) says it plainly, "No man can serve two masters: for either he will hate the one and love the other; or else. he will hold to the one, and despise the other, Ye cannot serve God and mammon." It's like thinking you can drive a car by looking at only the rear-view mirror instead of the windshield.

So, what does that mean? That if you simultaneously tend, desire, or support or devote yourself to two different— and usually conflicting—responsibilities, pursuits, ideas, or people it cannot end well. You flop back and forth, from this to that. Or you make a half commitment because it's hard to keep the full commitment. Take marriage for instance.

You are not married part time or alone. You are married together. If one spouse fails, it's hard for the other to keep going without the strength to endure the hardship or find the help to effect a change. If you are not serving The Master, it is very easy to become self-serving. And the stories change right along with it to support that choice.

When my two oldest son's marriages failed it was not for a lack of trying and could not say they did not know any better. A different master becomes a slippery slope that leads to a crooked path. And make no mistake, it is about choice and free will. After more than 15 years of marriage, they both threw it away. Most people married this long tend to be married for life. They were foolish.

Proverbs talks about fools 42 times! Being foolish must have meant something that it gets so many rich examples and references. <u>Proverbs 12:15</u> says, "The way of a fool is right in his own eyes, but a wise man listens to advice." The fool rejects the advice of others and instead listens only to himself.

In both marriages all of the husbands and wives must bear the responsibility for those choices that lead to divorces and broken homes. Fred and Sam's choices, like Rod's, had the worst impact on their children and the scars each and every one of them have carried into their adulthood. A little detour can be explained and corrected, but when you go off the cliff everyone is affected.

Coming from a Christian home, all of them knew and had a relationship with God. Thinking of my own family expectations I must have had my own head in the sand thinking my sons were stronger than they were.

You never know how your kids are going to change. That might be the biggest mystery of all. After Fred returned home from a Texas Christian college, he decided to get married. I looked at his life in the future and never saw the oncoming train of a habit he had begun much earlier. Most people think they can handle a habit until they cannot.

Habits are innocent at first. Then desire for more sets in. Something forbidden and inherently wrong. Eating a piece of pie is not going to do any harm, right? But what if you cannot stop eating? The piece of pie becomes the whole pie which has led to binging. Why have one drink when 10 will do? Just inhaling one time can lead to a lifetime habit. Poor health in the body, mind, and spirit permeates the relationships that were once healthy.

The more you try to quit, the more God continues to work on your conscience. It is not a mistake that your feelings began to increase your awareness that this habit must change. What stories will they listen to?

The change required means they must be willing to admit they have a problem and are willing to sacrifice that problem to save something greater. And it has to be something greater, or they will not change. If the change is not something they want, like the Energizer Bunny it will keep going. And going. And going. Their hidden habit is worn like a cloak of shame. Unable to stop it tears at the very fabric of the life they once lived.

Recovery is a second chance for everyone. If the desire is great enough, they will do it on their own. When my husband, Dutch, was diagnosed with cancer he quit smoking that day.

Not having the strength to change on our own, treatment and help is their salvation. This is God's gift of grace and mercy to all of us. We are assured in Hebrews 4:16 (NIV) Let us then approach the throne of grace with confidence, so that we may receive mercy and find grace to help us in our time of need.

Fred was given a second chance before he married Deborah. When confronted with his hidden alcohol and "dime bags" problems his future wife gave him the ultimate gift of mercy and sought treatment for him. A lesser person would have said it was his own problem. Together they were able to free him and build a strong relationship. Deborah never once complained he was not the perfect husband. Does one even exist? They have been happily married and serving the Lord in their ministries for 22 years.

Some are not so fortunate, including second son, Sam. He was a quiet and loving child, and he expressed that love to me throughout his life. Unfortunately, life's disappointments made it easier to avoid reality in his drugs and alcohol of choice. Never feeling appreciated for his talents he chose bitterness over victory. When he could have shown great appreciation to the brother that pulled him off a San Ysidro, CA hill he was living on, with no running water or electricity, he chose ridicule and humiliation of his brother. When his own children tried to demonstrate love he rebuked them. He seemed to revel in his misery, but it was a choice. His own son, Jason, said, "Not every day was a bad day but every day he woke up angry."

He loved the Lord and would profess his sorrow for his deeds, and eventually his sorrow became mine. Is it easier to lose another child? It's not easy with the first, or easier with the second or third. It grieves me to know he chose his lifestyle over life. When I could sleep, I would wake and grieve or cry for him, as I have done with all my losses. Psalms 46:10 (NIV) reminds us to "Be still and know that I am God." But for those that call upon the name of God, through Jesus Christ, they will never be left alone or be forsaken and will be lifted up. Only the strength of my hope and salvation in God, and my family, got me past this loss.

The seventh son was a joy. As a child, "Tiger" made everyone laugh. After my first husband passed away Dwayne may have lost his direction and certainly leadership. With all his older brothers gone, liquid courage replaced that gap. It would take twenty-five years to spiral out of control and a few more years to admit he needed help. He lost his business in Idaho, came back to California and lost another one. When people would say they saw my son on Palm Avenue I would cringe. He held a sign that said, "Only if you can, God bless you" as he begged for money and lived life as a "mountain man," a reference used by the homeless.

If he came by, he was fed but it tore me up to see his habit take its toll on him. He told me he begged for God's mercy to help him stop drinking. I was not sure if I believed this, but I continued to leave him a sandwich every day.

He wanted to take responsibility for getting control of his drinking habit and one morning asked me to take him to a clinic for help, which I obliged. I did not know how bad he had gotten but when he fell straight back and passed out cold on the floor he was in a severe seizure. The clinic attendant literally leapt over the counter and came to our aid. A gurney was there in seconds and whisked him off to the Coronado hospital, where he spent the next 10 days. The nerves in his legs were so damaged he could no longer walk on his own. The doctor said he had fallen so many times that any further falls would be permanent brain damage or death and his next drink would be his last one.

On the second day when I was allowed to see him, I called Linda and asked for her help to get him the help he needed. Linda and Dwayne have always been close, and I knew, at this point, he would be receptive to help. With all the research done, before Dwayne was released, we had found a rehab center we could afford that I knew would be his only hope. Most rehab centers will not take a recovering alcoholic until they have had 30 days clean sobriety. So, the first choice was a costly medical clinic. Was it worth it? Oh yes.

The second chance for Dwayne happened at Green Oaks Ranch in Vista, CA. It is a part time Bible camp and a fulltime recovery camp. There, Dwayne would have almost 30 days in recovery before he went AWOL and walked off the program.

When he arrived back at my home, I called Linda and put him on the phone with her. He assured her that he was, "on his road to recovery," and "Could do the rest on his own." At that, Linda's tough love told him to leave immediately and go do his recovery without our help.

Within a few weeks again I called Linda and put Dwayne on the phone. He was begging for help. The original slip into that alcohol-filled world was built over 25+ years. But the second chance comes with a real reality check. He said his fall was far faster than he could have realized and now knew he could not do this on his own. Spending the next 30 days on Linda's couch while he gained sobriety, she worked to get him back into Green Oaks. They did not want him. He had committed the cardinal sin and walked out of recovery. But we never gave up. Linda finally got Mary to take Dwayne's call, where he begged for forgiveness. When she said he did not have to beg, he said, "Yes Mary, I do. I am begging for forgiveness."

Dwayne spent the next nine months in this recovery program, putting in the work to make restitution, pay back fines and start the journey back to have the life he is living today. When he came out of the program, he asked Linda to go with him to meet Bill, to interview to rent a one room apartment. Bill would become his landlord in Coronado for the next 15 years. Dwayne put a sign on the bike he rode, advertising for work, as he sang, "I've got the joy, joy, joy, joy, down in my heart." Dwayne found his redemption through his sobriety. His daily walk of faith and reliance in Jesus Christ helped him build a life worth living. Today he has a successful business, fleet of trucks, purchased a second home, is active in his ministry and is enjoying his 15th year of sobriety. If you've ever tried to stop an addiction you have to speak victory to the outcome. What used to be a struggle gets easier as the path of the addiction is cut off.

A Friend of Bill's is a friend of Dwayne's, as he continues to express his recovery and testimony and second chance.

But for you, me, or the person trying to help, you have a lesson to learn too. It's the lesson in patience, enduring love, trust, obedience to God and discernment to know His will from yours. Help can easily become co-dependency as the lines of empathy and sympathy get blurred. Empathy has options, sympathy does not. Your desire to help may be overrun with, "I can't let them do that, I have to do something." Remember you can help, but you do not have to do it alone. And most likely, you must get help. Do not stop praying but get the right help. You cannot do everything, but you can do something.

Some people think a miracle is a starburst – a miraculous presentation of something that was not possible, but in a burst is presented to us or mankind. But this is what I know. The miracle of this period of my life is the understanding that true love of my children and the love of my Lord Jesus Christ has given me victory in my life as I rejoice in the spiritual rebirth of my children.

Through it all, God taught me my patience, perseverance and belief was strengthened by knowing I can "Be still and know that I am God" and that He is there for me 24/7. It is not a hoax, or a crutch, but my strength. Psalms 27:1 says it all that "The Lord is my strength and my salvation. For whom shall I be afraid?"

You'll Know Me By The Smile I'm Wearing

Then I saw "a new heaven and a new earth,"
for the first heaven and the first earth had
passed away, and there was no longer any sea.

Revelations 21:1 (NIV)

Chapter 25

You'll Know Me by the Smile I'm Wearing

Some people have asked me why, at 90, I wanted to write a book. It is not logical, they say. And I smile. A smile dispels many worries. And having a smile lets the sunshine in. It means hope to some, joy to others, and to others can be encouraging and inspiring. But there is no inspiration in logic. In fact, there is no courage or even happiness in logic. Just satisfaction. My daughter Linda said, "We can write a book in a few months!" It has now been a year into this journey. Clearly this was not an exercise in logic. But there is legacy, joy, and comfort in knowing that I am bringing hope to others and the encouragement that the struggle of life is worth it.

Looking at my life has been instructive. My ministry initially started out as a testimony of faith. It became testimony through my music. When I hear a good song, I smile from the inside out. Music surely is the soul's own speech. The curated songs at the beginning of the chapters were meant to share some of my joy I have felt through this journey. And now it is testimony through the legacy of my journey.

In the very first chapter of this book, we learn that looking forward, through the metaphorical windshield of our lives, gives us the widest view possible. While the rear-view mirror requires a look backwards, it also gives us the most perspective about what we just passed or went through. However, it is not meant to be our primary focus. For that reason, I do not look back on my life with regret or remorse. That is not to say that I have enjoyed every moment, but I have endured all of them, even the disappointments.

The purpose of this book for me, was to provide the reader with a glimpse of my lessons in the hope that it serves, not only as a testimonial, but as words to encourage you, and that you are not alone, nor do you face your challenges alone. It may seem like that at times, but I promise, you are not alone.

What is the meaning of life? It is *Not* about being happy! Happiness comes and goes. It is as much about setting goals, which helps us point our aim in a specific direction, as it is in setting limits. This requires discipline. In my early adulthood I had to learn this. We are not limitless, although thinking this way may temporarily get you through some challenges. Being responsible helps us understand that others depend on us and the lack of responsibility has a cause and maybe the unintended consequence of effects we do not want.

Mark Twain is credited with saying, "I have had many problems in my life, many of which have never happened." And the good humor found in those words encourages us to stop grumbling and complaining, engaging in a pity party for one or blaming others or circumstances for our perceived misfortune. Put prayer into your problems so you get through them faster.

What is truly remarkable is that we sometimes learn a lesson more than once. A lesson can be disguised as something you sort of triumphed over, yet it returns to teach us something completely different. In that lesson, maybe a death or a loss, we discover an opportunity that evolves into a blessing that was not obvious at the time.

And a lesson can even come back to test us or find out if we learned the lesson or not. I can think of a few examples but one that comes to mind is like getting a traffic ticket. Although you got caught, you did get not caught for all the previous infractions you know you got away with. The blessing that you were caught can teach you about the safety of others that would otherwise be risked by your recklessness or oversight.

Life requires us to be accountable. To God first and to our family second.

Each trial and test *are* meant to be a challenge, and you have to trudge your way through it, not around it. Some are easier, some are not. But total trust in God is the only way I have been able to live a life worth living and to be alive this long.

Second chances were mentioned as hope of a new tomorrow. I am grateful to have lived long enough to see the full redemption and recovery of two of my sons, while the separate loss of three other sons serves as a reminder of that grace, but I will always have a hole in my heart left by their passing.

I rejoice at this point in my life that I have the blessed company of four sons and two daughters. A few years back, after I turned 80, Linda caught me "faking" music reading. She would be the only one to detect that I could no longer read the notes in front of me. I confided that I was losing my sight. For the next few years together, we would battle the effect glaucoma had on my vision. As eyesight got worse, Linda or Fred would accompany me to the doctor. There the doctor would tell me he could not do anything…that I was going blind and that I would eventually be blind and never recover sight. When I would tell him that I expected and prayed for a miracle he would just laugh at me. In fact, each subsequent visit was taunted with, "Any miracles yet?" when I would greet him. The answer was always yes. Because I see in a completely different way now.

Being unsighted may not appear to be the best view, but this view has allowed me to see in a way that I would not have seen otherwise, because I can see by touch, sound and even a sixth sense of knowing how you feel.

Learning to *tune* inward has created another level of communication outward. And yes, I can even sense when someone is afraid that blindness is "contagious" or someone is fearful of being around someone with a handicap.

Initially being unsighted created total fear in me. Fear of what I could not see, fear of the unknown, fear of the loss of independence. And anger. Anger is just another version of fear. And believe me, I had to dig deeply to remember my strength and salvation was and still is my faith in Jesus Christ. My fear was faced gradually, and I remember when I began to recall the time, I looked at the desert's night sky. Not once did I look up at the sky and say there were too many stars. In the same way, I had to find other ways of seeing.

Little by little I began to trust those around me for my safety and even my food preparation. And I began to have a new appreciation for this. The opposite of fear is love. I replaced my fear with the love of being cared for. I encourage you to keep your courage strong, not your honor, glory, or pride. The people standing shoulder to shoulder with you have everything contained within, so trust them. Prove yourself worthy and stand with them.

Joy comes in the morning for me means there is light and hope. All the things that you will do this day starts in the morning. When you have cried or tarried in the night, joy and peace, even if momentary, is yours in the morning.

I started to count my blessings. Some mornings I would count more and more, and find the morning was already gone. Another blessing has been experiencing new life through the eyes of my 15 grandchildren and 16 great grandchildren.

At any point in your life, it is your outlook and faith that counts. And it will carry you through anything. We live a better life when we learn not to take our problems as seriously as we think they are. Get out of the way of receiving God's blessing and let go.

Keeping your mind intact is as important as minding your own business. There is less to be responsible for that way! Input determines output. So be careful about what goes into your mind.

Stay interested and curious in life. You will never live long enough to see or learn everything, but you will always be looking forward to it all.

And finally,

Be yourself. No one else can do that better. My journey has been a series of lessons shared in this book, but I want to leave you with some thoughts of what I have learned along the way.

I am going to run this race until God calls me home and I hear Him say, "well done."

Until we see each other, I will see you in the morning inside the Eastern Gate.

Miracles On Your Doorstep

The Ten Tenets

A new command I give you: Love one another. As I have loved you, so you must love one another.

John 13:34 (NIV)

Finale

The Ten Tenets

Honor

To God first, family second. Honor in God will encourage you one step at a time and keeps you looking forward to the goal and prize. Honor to your family means you will do right by them. There is a mighty power waiting to get out, so use it and be willing to be used.

Belief, Faith, and Commitment

Without these you will not have a big enough reason to honor whatever you have committed to. Being willing to adapt to less should not mean you do not have to do what is needed though. These three things helped me keep moving forward. They would also guide me to overcome challenges of despair, loneliness, and fear.

Trust

Trust goes hand in hand with belief, faith and commitment but adds 'without a doubt." Understand that $45 fed a family of nine for a whole week in 1965. Back then I only had $25. The point is I had to stop complaining about what I did not have to trust God to deliver what was needed. In turn I would learn to stop wasting and make what I did have work.

Forgiveness

Life well lived is not a life without mistakes. It is easier if you do not hold a grudge. Delete "you done me wrong" off your calendar so you do not celebrate the anniversary and remind the wrong doer. Put your faith in Jesus Christ and ask forgiveness. Let go and let God, then let it be.

Responsible

Life is easier when you decide if you are the pin or the cushion. This means take the lead and make the right choices. Then take responsibility for them and the outcome. Look forward to a second chance if you did not get it right the first time, but do not stop trying.

Truthful

It is thought that truth hurts. If it does find a way to deliver the same message with love and kindness but do not back down, whitewash it or dull it down. In any relationship, if you do not understand it is broken, it will not get fixed.

Hopeful

Staying focused on your past can keep you from seeing God's future. Look forward to it and remain prayerfully optimistic. What you believe is a disaster can be a gift.

Obedient

To God first. Don't be a secret agent for God. Surrender your will to His. Give of yourself as God gave of Himself. Selfless obedience reminds us to share kindness and be generous with our gifts.

Wisdom

It is an understanding or a knowing of something. The fear of the Lord is the beginning of knowledge, but fools despise wisdom and instruction (Prov 2.1 KJV)

Love

Be kind, helpful, thoughtful, going the extra measure, being contrite. Even asking for forgiveness. Learn to be helpful. Send a letter, pick up the phone, send an email. These things can lift and remind someone that they are loved, remembered and matter. Being relevant is a gift to give someone.

References

Introduction

1. Nicole Avant, *a recent interview about the current immigration crisis*.

Chapter 1

1. Dr. David Jeremiah, *Looking Forward* (This reference is from a CD that was recorded on 02/20/2020.)

Chapter 17

1. Dr. David Jeremiah, *The Jeremiah Study Bible* (Matthew 6:25 – 32)

2. Dr. David Jeremiah, *The Jeremiah Study Bible* (Matthew 6:33)

Chapter 23

1. Pastor Rick Warren, *Six Stages of Grief* (*https://revwords.com/6-stages-of-grief-rick-and-kay-warren/*)

About the Authors

Lorraine Snider-Hanley

As the first complete generation of immigrant parents, Lorraine is no stranger to challenges. From her preemie start in life, she faced obstacles that helped craft her place in life. She developed musical skills that helped her dodge teenagers' critical comments about her skin problems by becoming the sought-after musician she became. Seeking yet another remedy takes her on a remarkable journey most people would not have taken. Every door she opened led to another opportunity or challenge. But her faith never wavered. She overcame challenges that come with 81 months of pregnancy, built the largest piano student in a few years and was blessed with parenting nine children. Through it all, she even developed latent talents in oil painting, with many of her works commissioned. Most women would have retired but she just kept going, despite her eventually becomingtotally blind before she wrote this book. At 90, God has blessed this prayer warrior with longevity and clarity of mind.

About the Authors

Linda Kaye

Growing up the daughter of a lifelong entrepreneur, Linda's career as sales coach, real estate broker and #1 Best Selling author ("Rock Your Life"), leaves no doubt she has followed in her mother's footsteps. Linda's musical talents were nurtured by her mom and led to playing around the world as a musician and composer. Since early 2010 Linda has sold or leased over $500 Million dollars in Southern California Commercial Real Estate. She is CEO of a real estate lifestyle-change company, Open Roads, and shares her knowledge and sales skills in robust online courses. She volunteers in many community projects in Malibu, where she resides, and nurtures an abundant garden that attracts hundreds of hummingbirds.